The

Foundation

of Merit

Interpreting American Politics

Michael Nelson, Series Editor

The

Foundation

of Merit

Public Service in

American Democracy

Patricia Wallace Ingraham

The Johns Hopkins University Press

Baltimore and London

© 1995 The Johns Hopkins University Press

All rights reserved. Published 1995
Printed in the United States of America on acid-free paper
04 03 02 01 00 99 98 97 96 95   5 4 3 2 1

The Johns Hopkins University Press
2715 North Charles Street
Baltimore, Maryland 21218-4319
The Johns Hopkins Press Ltd., London

A catalog record for this book is available from the British Library.

Library of Congress Cataloging-in-Publication Data

Ingraham, Patricia W.
    The foundation of merit : public service in American democracy / Patricia Wallace
Ingraham.
        p.   cm.—(Interpreting American politics)
Includes bibliographical reference and index.
ISBN 0-8018-5111-4 (hc : alk. paper).—ISBN 0-8018-5112-2 (pbk. : alk. paper)
1. Civil service—United States—History.   2. Bureaucracy—United States—His-
tory.   3. Civil service reform—United States—History.   I. Title.   II. Series.
JK681.I53   1995
350.4'0973—dc20   95-14309

For the memory of my father
and
for my mother

Contents

Series Editor's Foreword

Consider this list of connotations that, according to a leading college textbook, many Americans associate with the word *bureaucracy*: flabby, overpaid, and lazy; unimaginative; intolerably meddlesome; a demanding leviathan; slow to abandon unsuccessful policies and accept new ideas; arrogant, smug, and condescending; impersonal; red-tape artists; social engineers; intrusive empire builders; devoted to rigid procedures.

What are we to make of this list? First, and most obviously, it is unrelievedly negative. One would be hard-pressed to tease a positive connotation out of the popular imagination, even though most people report that their personal encounters with specific bureauratic agencies are positive. Second, the list is rich in contradiction, Who is the villain —the "flabby, overpaid, and lazy" time-server who spends the day reading the sports page, or the zealous "social engineer" who wakes up thinking of new ways to tell other people how to live their lives?

Contradictions such as these beset American bureaucracy, but the one that concerns Patricia Wallace Ingraham the most is between the merit system, whose purported virtue is its removal of politics from the hiring, firing, and promoting of civil servants, and democratic politics, which in the actual case has always dominated the merit system. The contradiction has existed since the moment of conception: the Pendleton Act of 1883, which created the merit system, also empowered the president to decide how broad the system's coverage should be, thus assuring that such decisions would be made according to political criteria and that the system would never follow the British practice of including high-level executives

Not surprisingly, the United States has more political appointees in its national bureaucracy than any other western government—around 3,000, compared with 120 in Great Britain and 40 in Germany, for example. These officials, who are appointed as agents of the president, typically regard the merit civil service, especially the mid-level managers with whom they deal most frequently, as a beast to be tamed or (depending on the stereotype to which the appointees subscribe) awakened. By the time they leave office (often in a year or two), they may think differently, but by then the opportunity to work together constructively with their merit system colleagues is gone.

Ingraham's account of the foundations of merit is not one of black-hatted political appointees versus white-hatted civil servants, however. Because the civil service has evolved such complex rules and regulations to govern itself (usually the product of political appointees' efforts to bring it under control!), mid-level managers can thwart political direction by finding sanctuary in the rules' manifold inconsistencies. A more serious problem is that the merit system promotes people to management positions not on the basis of their managerial skills or training but, rather, because of their technical competence in a specialized area.

Democratic politics has come into conflict with the merit system in other ways, according to Ingraham. The preference in hiring which veterans have enjoyed since the Civil War, along with the recent preference for minorities and women, has placed claims of right above claims of merit. In addition, the trend toward "contracting out" government services to private firms has diluted the role of civil servants in the business of government.

Ingraham offers several helpful suggestions for meliorating the contradictions between democratic politics and the merit system. But melioration, not resolution, is all that can reasonably be hoped for. Underlying all the visible contradictions are two more fundamental ones: the contradiction between constitutional democracy and the unelected governmental power that bureaucracy wields, and the contradiction between the bureaucratic agency's commitment to procedure and regularity and the political official's desire for rapid change.

Michael Nelson

Preface

and

Acknowledgments

In 1988, when the late, and still deeply missed, Charlie Levine asked me to serve as a staff member for the National Commission on the Public Service (the Volcker Commission), I readily agreed. I thought I understood the civil service system and its problems; I had studied past reforms and thought I understood them as well. I quickly found that I had a great deal to learn. However, as the work of the Task Force on Recruitment and Retention began, its excellent chair, Rocco Siciliano, and I discovered that much of the information and data we needed to answer our questions did not exist. Answers to straightforward questions—How many ways are there to hire in the federal government?—were difficult to find and were often contradictory when we did discover them. We found ourselves relying on sporadic and anecdotal data more often than not. Simply describing the complexity of the system was a daunting task; we became even more convinced that it was an important one.

This murky system and its accompanying maze of laws, rules, and regulations is a cornerstone of effective governance. If it does not work, neither does government. The civil service system—the bureaucracy—serves as the critical link between the institutions of government and the citizens they serve. In an important sense, it represents those citizens as well. It is called on to support the exploration of space, the disposal of radioactive waste, the provision of clean air and water, the timely distribution of Social Security benefits, and the national defense, among many other tasks, both simple and complex. Why has it so frequently been a target of political rhetoric and reform? How has it become so difficult to understand?

There are several answers to these questions. Most depend on the inherently political nature of the "neutral" civil service, the power it has inevitably and inexorably accrued, and the relationship between temporary elected officials and the members of the permanent bureaucracy. Despite the long-term efforts of theorists and practicing public servants to remove political issues from the operation of the civil service, an understanding of the continuing role of politics—both "high politics" and "low politics," in Don Kettl's terms—is fundamental to understanding the system. Too often, changes or reforms in the civil service have been described as "technical" or "managerial" in both intent and impact. They are not and they cannot be. The system was created as a political compromise; it grew at the expense of patronage; it has been reformed for explicitly political purposes; the outcomes of reform have had political impact.

It is the intent of this book to place the federal public service—the merit system—firmly in the context of the politics and the history that have created its complexity. That history begins at the founding of the nation; one of the continuing issues for the contemporary merit system is its proper place in governance. The system developed with the state. The many tensions it includes reflect the changing values, changing politics, and changing patterns of participation in the United States. This was not a tidy process; it is not surprising that the system that the process produced is equally messy.

The book describes the evolution of the merit system in some detail. It does so because no major add-on to the civil service has been subsequently eliminated. Whatever their initial purpose, these additions to the system continue to have significant implications for its current operation. To understand why some things do not work as anticipated, it is important to understand that they were created for a different time, to solve a different problem. Now they are creating new problems.

The book concludes with a discussion of the changing nature of government work and government workers, and the changing face of reform efforts. In nations around the world, new economic constraints and altered expectations for government have produced new methods of delivering government services and demands for more flexible and innovative public institutions. The centralized and standardized structures of most civil service systems cannot meet these new demands. The rapid pace of technological progress and the concomitant demands for new levels of expertise and technical knowledge have had a profound impact on government; again, the old systems have not met the challenge. The final chapter of the book examines the new realities of reform: they must be based on a clear understanding of what did not work in the past, but also on a coherent theory of change in public organizations and the critical role that politics and elected officials will play in that change.

I am indebted to a number of people for support and assistance in writing this book. Dean John Palmer and Bunny Jump, chair of the Department of Public Administration at Syracuse University's Maxwell School of Citizenship and Public Affairs, provided a semester off to get the project under way. Maxwell also provided two outstanding research associates, Jim Thompson and Dale Jones, whose assistance was invaluable. Diane Miller, the department's administrative assistant, helped the book escape from the computer and smiled while she did so. The students in my Maxwell seminars provided insights and analyses that were unfailingly useful. Discussions with good friends and colleagues—Rosemary O'Leary, Barbara Romzek, Don Kettl, Paul Light, Brint Milward, and Guy Peters—were tremendously useful as I sorted through thoughts and ideas. I also had the good fortune to work with exceptional public servants who, as Woodrow Wilson would say, "straightened my path." I am indebted to Ron Sanders, Sally Marshall, Roz Kleeman, and Al Zuck for that.

My most profound thanks are to my wonderful and patient family— our daughters Erin and Molly, and my husband, Charlie—for whose love, support and friendship I am thankful every single day. Erin and Molly are wonderful young women whose adventures and perspectives on life make us proud and happy, and keep us on our toes. Charlie is my best friend and an important partner in all that I do. He was a saint while I was working on this book.

Introduction

Civil service systems have three basic purposes: they permit governments to recruit qualified personnel for public jobs; they reward and develop the public workforce; and they provide guidelines or rules for organizing that workforce to meet public objectives. The systems are part of government, however, and often serve other purposes as well. As civil service systems and other governmental institutions have evolved together in many countries, the purposes of the civil service have meshed with the broader objectives of government: to represent and be responsive to the citizenry, and to serve elected officials, for example. The fit between traditional civil service objectives and those of the government as a whole is not always comfortable. It illuminates an important point about civil service systems, however: their design and operation describe a national view of government and the role of government in society.

As the public service evolved with the other institutions of government in the United States, critical decisions about design were made. Many of those decisions reflected major political movements and trends. Widespread patronage was linked to mass democracy and to populism, as was the strong reliance on simple common sense as the basic qualification for public jobs. This latter emphasis deviated sharply from the common European pattern of entry to the public service through elite institutions of higher education.

The politics of "good government" in the mid-1800s was largely responsible for introducing the rather antiseptic concept of neutral competence to the American federal service. Politics more generally provided the justification for the incremental way in which merit and neutral competence replaced patronage. The passage of the first civil service legislation, the Pendleton Act, in 1883, was not a rejection of the overt politicization of the federal service. It was, rather, a classic political solution to the problems that patronage posed: merit would be introduced, but slowly, and through executive orders of the president, rather than through legislative action. Politics and merit became legally, institutionally, and inextricably entwined.

As it has developed, the civil service system, designed to cover 10 percent of the existing workforce in 1883, expanded to cover most federal employees. Because it expanded incrementally and generally at the will of the president, however, the civil service system—or the merit system, as it is often called—could grow only in competition with, and at the expense of, the political patronage system it was intended to correct. From the beginning, the relationship between the civil service on the one hand and elected officials and their appointees on the other was not a partnership, but an association filled with wary antagonism. It is not surprising, then, that the "merit" the system was intended to create and protect has become a frequent target of political criticism. At the same time, the role of the civil service and its power in government have grown larger.

The New Deal, World War II, and a generally prosperous and expanding economy in the postwar years created new tasks and responsibilities for government. The civil service system was central to the government's ability to deliver new and more complicated services. The Great Society policies of the 1960s increased the demands even further; health, education, poverty, and housing programs were created and implemented. Government agencies and personnel were asked and expected to explore space, to conduct critically important medical research, and to pursue the rights and freedoms promised by civil rights legislation. Later, environmental concerns about clean air, clean water, the safe disposal of hazardous waste, and cleaner and safer fuels added to the federal policy and program agenda. The role of the civil service and the characteristics and skills of its personnel had to change dramatically to meet these new demands. They did not always do so satisfactorily.

Failure to perform satisfactorily, however, did not result in immediate change, or, in some cases, in any change at all. There are several reasons for this. The public organizations that civil service systems support and reinforce are often large bureaucratic institutions. Bureaucracies do not change easily in any circumstances. When such structures are reinforced by the legal procedures and constraints of civil service laws and rules, and by the rigid hierarchy of classification systems, change is even more difficult. Public organizations and the civil service systems that supported them became extremely stable entities. The organizations, their programs, and their employees were able to outlast political cycles, elections, and leaders. Although bureaucratic expertise was increasingly central to public problem solving, it was also increasingly removed from external perspective and direction.

In the United States, dissatisfaction with government and the performance of its institutions increased dramatically in the 1960s. President Richard Nixon, convinced that he had inherited a permanent bureaucracy wedded to the ideas and programs of the Great Society, proposed a series of changes to restructure and reorganize the federal government. Watergate cut short that effort at reform, but the issue remained on the agenda. In his 1976 presidential campaign, Jimmy Carter argued that civil service reform was necessary because merit had disappeared. "There is no merit in the merit system," he said.

Carter was successful in obtaining passage of comprehensive civil service reform, the first since the Pendleton Act had created the merit system in 1883. The Civil Service Reform Act of 1978 was intended to make the civil service, particularly at the top levels of management, more flexible, more responsive, and more productive. The Civil Service Commission was abolished and new agencies were created to help with that task.

Ten years after the reform, however, the director of the Office of Personnel Management, one of the new agencies created by Carter's reform, declared that the civil service system remained burdened by thousands of pages of rules and regulations and did not work. Additional reforms were undertaken; training and development were reemphasized and compensation was made less standard. As the twenty-first century approaches, fundamental reforms are on the agenda. In his campaign and in the first years of his presidency, President Clinton declared government to be "broke and broken," and advocated the complete "reinvention" of government. The civil service system still is not fixed. Why not?

Civil Service Systems: What Are the Issues?

Many of the recurring problems with civil service systems are related to one fundamental point: they are not just about personnel rules and regulations. Civil service systems are integral parts of government and the site of a critical interface between government and its citizens. They provide and support the people who permit government to carry out public programs and policies.

They are also products of constitutional, political, economic, and social demands and decisions. Not all of these decisions are tidy and clear-cut. Many are compromises and contain conflicting objectives and views of the civil service. Many are decisions born in the democratic and political environment of the civil service system and overlaid on its basic purposes. The following highlights some of the most important tensions and conflicts that result.

Patronage versus Merit

Patronage versus merit is the most basic and the most persistent issue for the American civil service. The increasingly blatant patronage systems of the nineteenth century had two negative results: they eliminated virtually all criteria for public office except political affiliation, and they destabilized government by sweeping out large numbers of employees after each election. The combination not only devalued public service but led to serious inefficiencies and lack of competence.

To some extent, this was caused by the nature of the American state. The institutions of government did not grow and develop with the state. The state emerged full-blown from the Revolution; its institutions developed as the demand for government services grew. The public bureaucracy emerged from the same group that produced the first elected officials and active citizens: the wealthy landowners. Patronage meant the appointment of friends and acquaintances with similar backgrounds, educations, and perspectives.

As the state developed and as political parties and political participation became more broadly based, patronage changed as well. Office seekers flooded the capital after each election, advertising in the newspapers for public jobs and pursuing them through every available political contact. Andrew Jackson is the president most often associated with the excesses of patronage, but he did not expand patronage any more than did many presidents before and after him.

From the time of the Jackson presidency until the passage of the Pendleton Act, however, the problem of patronage was increasingly on the public agenda. Advocates of good government argued that politics had to be removed from the daily operation of government if public programs were to be effectively administered. They did not argue that any particular skills were necessary for this good administration, only that partisan political considerations had to be removed from entrance into the public service.

What made sense to the reformers, however, did not make so much sense to politicians. Patronage served an important purpose in building parties and in maintaining partisan loyalty. For presidents and members of Congress anxious to be reelected, the removal of the ability to award public jobs meant the loss of a strong source of political influence. Further, as the government matured and as the bureaucracy grew, presidents increasingly believed that they needed political appointees inside public organizations to maintain some level of control.

The American civil service emerged as a kind of hybrid. The career civil service forms the largest part of public organizations, but at the top levels of the organizations are political appointees. The political executives serve as presidential messengers and managers of policy direction and change. The United States has the largest number of political appointees of any major Western nation, and those numbers have increased substantially in the past twenty years. The larger numbers are not signs of success, however. Rather, they indicate that the tensions created by placing political appointees and career civil servants in the same organizations and expecting them to work together as well-oiled units have never been resolved. Indeed, the issue of political management of the permanent bureaucracy has been a major problem for every president in the last quarter of a century.

Neutrality versus Responsiveness

Neutrality versus responsiveness is closely related to patronage and merit. Simply put, the problem is this: if a civil service system is created to insulate the public service from political excesses, how is it possible to guarantee that the service is still responsive to legitimate political direction? The problem is further complicated by the ongoing debate between the Congress and the president regarding the direction of the career civil service. Failure to resolve this debate has led to a tug-of-war and frequently conflicting directions for and expectations of the civil service.

Initially, the problem was addressed theoretically, and to some extent practically, by attempts to separate politics completely from administration. Administration would be the domain of neutral experts whose application of skills and knowledge to public services would be unfettered by political considerations, but who would be completely responsive to political directives. Herbert Kaufman likened this neutral civil service to a "hammer or saw" that could be used for any purpose.

In a democratic system, this neutrality is key to a legitimate role in government for the civil service. As elections shift partisan control of the presidency and Congress, both parties must be confident that the members of the civil service will respond to new policy directions. Two developments in modern government have undermined that confidence. First, the growth of government has created large central bureaucracies whose structures and operating procedures isolate them from external influence and direction. Second, the increasing complexity of public programs and policies has caused bureaucratic expertise to be at once more esoteric and more central to decision making about public policy. The larger role played by bureaucratic actors in policy, coupled with the stability provided by civil service rules and regulations, has caused renewed concern about political direction of public bureaucracies and civil servants.

Much of the modern relationship between the president and the permanent bureaucracy involves presidential efforts to tighten control over the decisions of career civil servants. Franklin Roosevelt created entire agencies outside the civil service laws, announcing that what he needed was not neutral competence, but policy experts whom he could trust. Dwight Eisenhower created a new group of political appointees to increase his policy control, and Richard Nixon and Ronald Reagan designed elaborate management strategies to improve political direction of the bureaucracy. Jimmy Carter did not characterize the civil service as a hammer or saw, but rather as the "giant Washington marshmallow" that simply absorbed all attempts to direct and control it.

An additional issue is raised by the efforts of political executives to direct public bureaucracies. As the civil service system became increasingly insular, the link between management and the civil service system became tenuous. Line managers did not recruit or hire their employees; the central personnel office did that. The ways in which a manager could discipline her employees were largely determined by personnel rules and regulations, and discipline was often handled by a personnel office. Total numbers of employees were controlled by the Office of Management and Budget (OMB); total budgets were determined by the OMB and Congress. Managers were left with limited flexibility and discretion, isolated in important ways from both those they managed and supervised and those who wanted to manage them.

For those at the top of the career service pyramid, the members of the Senior Executive Service, the picture was complicated by their relationship with the political executives who theoretically directed the agency for which they worked. The career executives were to serve as senior managers for the career civil service and as links between that service and political appointees; they were also to act as policy advisors and "organizational experts" for the appointees. They were to assist the appointees, who often served in one position only for a brief time, in understanding the complexity of public organizations and their accompanying rules and regulations. These different responsibilities created a difficult situation for the career executives. To the extent that they were perceived to be acting in the interests of the career civil servants they managed, they were often distrusted by the political executives to whom they reported. To the extent that they were perceived to be too responsive to political executives by the civil servants they managed, career executives were distrusted by their employees. The foundation for an effective network that includes political executives, career executives, and other members of the career civil service is, at best, difficult to create.

The collision of different perspectives and objectives, different time frames and lengths of service, and different understandings of the environment in which public management occurs precluded an effective partnership between the key members of the public management team. The escalating political rhetoric directed at the permanent bureaucracy in the 1980s eroded the foundation further. The creation of a constructive relationship, a partnership for effective government, is a major challenge for the future.

Efficiency versus Effectiveness

Another recurring dilemma for the American civil service has been how to ensure efficient operation while still responding to diverse objectives and directives. The early call for neutrality addressed this issue. Because neutral competence would exclude politics, decisions would be rational and resources could be used for maximum efficiency. This assumed, of course, that directions were clear and solutions simple. As the reality of government challenged this assumption, it became clear that efficiency was often only one of many objectives pursued by governmental agencies.

Efforts to pursue it, however, are an important part of the history of the American civil service. The private sector has often provided a model for how government organizations should operate, and reform efforts have often been guided by private-sector principles. The scientific management movement, described in chapter 3, is a classic, but certainly not an isolated, example. There has also been a concern with determining and measuring the products or outcomes of government agencies and employees. Absent the bottom line that allows performance measurement in private corporations, public organizations have struggled with measures of efficiency and productivity. These issues have become more central as the costs of government have escalated and attempts to control them have become more numerous.

Effectiveness has been nearly as elusive. Because many government programs address complex and multidimensional problems (the provision of decent housing or adequate health care, for example), the determination of effective service-delivery strategies and the long-term difference they make is difficult. Effectiveness may also be viewed as serving multiple clients or interests satisfactorily. Multiple clients, however, mean multiple demands, multiple perspectives on "satisfactory" service delivery, and multiple definitions of effectiveness. Further, trade-offs with efficiency are inevitable.

Who Cares?

The complexity of these issues demonstrates the depth and the tenacity of the challenges confronting civil service systems and those who would reform them. But why does it matter? It matters for two reasons: first, without an effective civil service, a government is not able to deliver critical programs and services to its citizens. Civil service systems recruit and reward the people who ensure that Social Security checks are delivered on time, that critical safety standards are maintained, and that fundamental rights are preserved. An effective civil service is absolutely critical to effective government.

Second, public organizations and civil service systems are powerful actors in the public policy process. Methods for directing and using that power constructively are not easy to find, and past efforts provide little solace. The president increases the total number of political appointees and enlarges the White House staff; the Congress creates its own bureaucracy; the courts become increasingly involved in bureaucratic decision making and the daily activities of public organizations. Bureaucratic power remains strong, more rules are added, and the problem is exacerbated.

There is no question that major reforms will come. Most civil service systems are products of the nineteenth century. They are ill suited to meet the needs of the twenty-first. They do not describe contemporary realities of government; they are not structured to be problem-solving entities; they do not operate from a foundation based on the trust of citizens and elected officials. It is the intent of this book to describe significant developments in the history of the American federal civil service; more importantly, this book aims to place the civil service in the context of American government and politics and to consider how, and if, the public service can again become a legitimate partner in the enterprise of governance.

The

Foundation

of Merit

Chapter One

Civil Service Systems

and

Government

The Critical Links

Public personnel systems are often described in negative terms; they are seen as sterile, mechanical organizations that create seas of faceless bureaucrats consumed by procedure and routine. At best, they are described as sets of rules and regulations whose purpose is to provide a neutral and objective public hiring process. The reality of the systems, however, is both more complex and more profound. Public personnel systems— or merit systems or civil service systems—are about governance and good government. They hire, motivate, discipline, and reward the government employees who are the most immediate and visible link between the institutions of government and the citizens they serve. Civil service systems create the repositories of skills and expertise that permit governments to address pressing problems and needs. They are meant to be dedicated to the public interest and to serving the public good, broadly defined.

Public personnel systems are also about power, politics, and the inevitable tension between large bureaucratic institutions and elected officials. Dwight Waldo observes in *The Administrative State* that administrative theory necessarily includes political theory.[1] Others have argued that the development of administrative institutions is closely related to political movements and ideas, sometimes in unpredictable ways.[2] Michael Nelson contends, in fact, that "at almost every critical turn in American bureaucratic history, the efforts of public officials and organized political groups to enhance popular control of government inadvertently planted the seeds of modern bureaucratic power."[3]

Administration and politics are both blatantly and subtly intertwined. Many key issues in the history of civil service institutions relate to the limitations they place on elected officials' desire for patronage and other perquisites of office. Other issues concern the ability of the institutions supported and protected by civil service systems to accrue, wield, and protect power of their own. Not surprisingly, much of the history of the civil service is about how that power can be controlled by the president, the courts, the Congress, and citizens. Many contemporary problems are rooted in the same relationships.

The point that, at their core, civil service systems are fundamentally connected to politics is central to an understanding of both the significance and the operation of most modern systems. The elimination or constraint of political patronage did not remove politics from merit. Rather, it created one of the most enduring tensions in the American political system. It is natural and legitimate for elected officials to direct the activities of public organizations. Without question, merit systems make that more difficult. They protect most hiring from political influence; they protect public employees from arbitrary firing; they create rules and institutional boundaries that limit the influence of elected officials in many ways.

Efforts to reassert political influence—to limit the independent power of public bureaucracies—are a hallmark of American politics. In many cases, as Nelson suggests, the "solutions" have become the new problems. When the civil service system was created, for example, a substantial role for patronage was retained. Merit advanced against politics only by executive order of the president. As the leader of his party, the president had the most to lose by circumscribing patronage. Most leaders of Western democracies exercise limited patronage authority, but the president of the United States assumes a major appointment task when he takes office. Filling all the available slots with qualified personnel has become a serious issue for the contemporary presidency; keeping appointees in place and managing the truncated organizations created by this solution have become increasingly difficult tasks as well.[4]

It is important to understand how closely developments in the evolution of public personnel have reflected national political movements and the priorities and values they represent. The elitist early view of public service—it was to be composed of "gentlemen" like themselves, as Frederick Mosher notes[5]—reflected limited political participation and founding values. Stephen Skowronek and others have observed that the widespread patronage of the 1800s reflected emerging mass participation in partisan politics; when civil service legislation was passed, the emphasis in the first civil service laws on commonsense principles, wide geographic access to examining centers, and open competition for jobs responded to the same influence.[6]

By reflecting politics in this way, and by combining the clutter and flux of politics with the reason and rigidity of bureaucracy, the American federal civil service achieved and retained a level of legitimacy. The trade-offs, however, often carried substantial costs. The American civil service is one of the most rule driven in the world. When accountability to elected officials is questioned (and it often is), accountability to rules is strengthened and held in high regard. The paradox is that layers upon layers of rules do not ensure control or accountability. They may, in fact, increase bureaucratic power and discretion by providing so many rules that not all can reasonably be followed.[7]

Although the United States presents an extreme case, the conundrum of effective direction and control of civil service systems is one of concern to most modern democracies. As government problems have become more complex, and particularly as government resources have become more constrained, civil service systems have become targets of change and reform efforts around the world. Major reforms have been implemented in Great Britain, the Netherlands, Australia, New Zealand, and Canada, to name only the leading examples.[8] What are the sources of the problems and why are they so widespread?

The Issue of Bureaucratic Power

Bureaucratic structures and civil service systems are not synonymous, but they have many characteristics that are mutually reinforcing. Both are rigid, inflexible, and closed; both were designed, in fact, to exclude external influences. For bureaucratic structures, the goal was to maximize efficient use of skills and expertise.[9] For civil service systems, the goal was to maximize neutrality in the hiring, compensation, and promotion of their members. The greatest commonalities between them are the closed boundaries, the reliance on hierarchical authority, and the use of standardized rules and regulations to guide internal activities. Both civil service systems and bureaucratic structures are created to be stable, predictable, and long-lasting. Both guard and insulate knowledge and expertise.[10] There are good reasons for adopting both. Large organizations require structure to retain coherence. There are some routine tasks that are best performed in a stable and predictable way, and there are many cases in which bureaucratic organizations effectively use and retain expertise to solve important public problems.[11]

Civil service systems were seen as fundamental to a return to "good government" in the United States; the order and stability they imposed on what had become a chaotic situation was seen as a public good. Furthermore, the neutrality that civil service systems were designed to ensure was a necessary corrective to political favoritism.

Neither bureaucratic structure nor civil service procedure is neutral, however. Harold Seidman and Robert Gilmour, while discussing organizational options, explicitly argue that when these rigid structures are adopted in a public setting, "we are making decisions with significant political implications." [12]

One of those implications has to do with the gradual accretion of power in bureaucratic institutions. There are numerous reasons for this accretion. Some concern the nature of the government itself. There are many grey areas and ambiguities in the American Constitution. Checks and balances, the separation of powers, and other constitutional provisions have created power voids and potential stalemates in the federal government. Bureaucracy does not tolerate ambiguity; the task of its procedures is to standardize and categorize. It is also in the nature of bureaucratic institutions to expand and to incorporate new tasks and activities into bureaucratic routine.

Other reasons for increased bureaucratic power have to do with the public policy process and the political decisions that influence it. Theodore Lowi and others have observed that the political process has steadily moved away from difficult decisions. Compromise and the accompanying blurring of objectives, the inclusion of conflicting goals in programs and policies, and a mandate to do more than available funds will permit are common factors in political decisions. The language of legislation is often remarkably unclear; members of the permanent bureaucracy exercise extensive discretion in imposing clarity on such imprecision.[13] This contributes in important ways to bureaucratic power in the implementation process.[14]

The extensive involvement of bureaucratic actors in other public policy activities adds another dimension to bureaucratic power. The bureaucracy's role as a repository of expertise and institutional memory for past policy experience is important here; when new policies are created or old ones redesigned, expert civil servants often play a central part in problem definition, analysis of alternative solutions, and evaluation of past efforts.[15]

The remarkable stability of bureaucratic institutions also enhances their ability to acquire power in a governmental setting. In a political system that is constantly in flux, in which electoral cycles provide the time frame for policy choice and action, the longevity and expertise of members of the permanent bureaucracy become important bargaining chips. That longevity also permits the formation of lasting ties with citizen and interest groups and with members of Congress and their staffs. The "iron triangles" thus created become important centers of pooled power and significant influences on public policy.[16]

There is a tradition in public administration that argues that public bureaucracies should not and do not exercise independent power; the "politics-administration dichotomy," first suggested by Woodrow Wilson in 1887, bases the legitimacy of the civil service and public bureaucracy on their responsiveness to power wielded by elected officials.[17] The reality of complex contemporary problems and the role of government in trying to solve them, as well as the other influences noted above, have inevitably enhanced bureaucratic power, however. Frederick Mosher provides an elegant summary of the dilemma this poses:

> The accretion of specialization and of technological and social complexity seems to be an irreversible trend, one that leads to increasing dependence upon the protected, appointive public service, thrice removed from direct democracy. Herein lies the central and underlying problem . . . how can a public service so constituted be made to operate in a manner compatible with democracy?[18]

There are different answers to this question and they create visions of completely different public service systems. One vision is that of a public service integrated into governance, with a clear sense of its democratic and constitutional responsibilities, marked by personal accountability and widely held ethical norms.[19] This vision of the public service is modeled to some extent on the European higher civil services: cadres of respected career civil servants who serve key policy functions across elections and changes of political parties and whose legitimate function in government is widely accepted.[20] This model can be found in the higher civil service in France; in that nation members of the elite higher service also frequently move from civil service posts into political positions and back again. The model was also found in the pre-Thatcher British civil service; since the Thatcher government, however, the role of the higher civil service in Great Britain has been significantly diminished.[21]

The second view is the more widely held in the United States and is reinforced by the provisions and constraints of the civil service system; it clearly demonstrates the traditional reliance on hierarchy and structure.

This vision was succinctly summarized by Donald Devine, who headed the Office of Personnel Management (OPM) early in the Reagan administration: "The skill and technical expertise of the career service must be utilized, but it must be utilized under the direct authority and personal supervision of the political leader who has the moral authority flowing from the people through an election."[22] In this model, accountability occurs only through responsiveness to political leaders and through compliance with the rules and regulations designed to limit bureaucratic discretion and authority. It is an essentially Weberian view of public organizations.

The Clinton administration's proposals for "reinventing government" provide a dramatically different view of public organizations and public employees. The emphasis on smaller, flatter, more discretionary organizations suggests much less opportunity for political appointees to exert clear authority. This is especially true in terms of the emphasis placed on customer service—on being responsive to those served by the program. Opening the boundaries of the organization is necessary, as is creating mechanisms that ensure accountability to the various customer groups served by the organization's programs and activities. Internal political mechanisms become only one (essentially undefined) part of the accountability mosaic.[23]

There is yet another perspective, one that is not so fixed. Herbert Kaufman argues that three primary values are built into and drive the American federal civil service. The first, the emphasis on economy or efficiency, grew from the early years of the civil service and from the influences of the private-sector mass-production line. Theorists of scientific management and others argued that, because much government activity was routine, it was possible to find the best way to perform each task most efficiently and for the least cost and to replicate that way across government. Theorists such as Luther Gulick argued that efficiency was the "number one value" in government.[24]

The second major value, responsiveness, refers to the responsiveness of the civil service to elected officials. Although this applies to both the president and the Congress, since the publication of the Brownlow committee report in 1937, which argued that the president was the "center of energy" in the executive branch, responsiveness has increasingly been identified with responsiveness to presidential direction and control.[25] Efforts by presidents and their staffs to achieve this responsiveness have marked virtually every administration since that of Franklin Roosevelt.

The third value is somewhat more nebulous. Effectiveness generally means effectively meeting democratic goals such as the equitable provision of services and the balancing of the many demands placed on public organizations by their diverse constituents. Effectiveness also includes the effort to represent the society and effectively consider the diverse viewpoints that are suggested in that process. As the brief discussion of the reinvention model above suggests, definitions of effectiveness must now include the ability to be flexible and innovative and to perform satisfactorily from the customer's point of view. Clearly, this is a potentially contradictory and troublesome set of definitions.

Kaufman argues that the interplay of these values should be seen as a cycle, with one or two ascending in significance while the third becomes less important. The cyclical nature of the interplay, however, ensures that the character of the civil service is dynamic and most often in flux.[26] The cycle also suggests that consensus about the proper and legitimate role for the civil service is, at best, fleeting. The unstable world that this creates is made even more unsteady by the unresolved issues related to the exercise of bureaucratic power.

Politics and the Public Service

One of the fundamental dilemmas confronting modern government is how to balance partisan politics and the institutions of the state. Politics—popular participation in government through parties and elections—is an integral part of democratic systems. It can also be a troubling presence, however. The positive qualities of citizen membership and participation in the system are sometimes offset by the abuse of political power, by the exclusion of some groups of citizens, and by the tendency to concentrate power in the hands of a few elected officials or interest groups. Modern issues of congressional reform, revitalization of parties, and improved voter education and participation are all related to these problems.

For the merit system, the problem with politics is somewhat different. There is no question that the civil service system and the public employees within it should be responsive to political direction. The civil service is, as Mosher noted, thrice removed from elections. On the other hand, the merit system was devised in the United States precisely because elected officials abused their responsibility to govern effectively. When the merit system was created, politics was the evil that the reformers intended to correct. Merit was viewed in terms of good government, as opposed to that influenced by politics.

The dilemma is immediately clear: how is merit to offset the evil of politics, but still respond to its legitimate authority? The problem has been consistently addressed, but never solved. The politics-administration dichotomy (or, at least, the separation of one from the other) was one early proposal for resolving the tension. Woodrow Wilson observed that it would be possible for administration to "straighten the path of government" if administrators remained above politics, and simply used their administrative skills and techniques to implement political decisions.[27] The added benefit of this approach was that administrators could be efficient because their activities would not be complicated and attenuated by political distractions. The development of the dichotomy between politics and administration in the United States is discussed in greater detail below.

The realities of modern government and the significant role of public organizations and civil servants in public policy processes, however, have made a dichotomous view of the relationship between politics and the merit system increasingly inaccurate (although, as the quotation above from Devine indicates, certainly not dead!). The critical part public institutions and their employees play in governing and governance has been widely discussed and documented, but the legitimacy these functions suggest for public bureaucracies remains elusive.[28]

Indeed, many efforts to replace the dichotomy fall back on its fundamental themes without suggesting a resolution for the underlying conflict. Some of the reinvention efforts of the Clinton administration, for example, are in this category. One principle of reinvention, to steer, rather than row, is a case in point.[29] This principle specifically suggests that members of the career civil service assume a policy and leadership role that was clearly reserved for elected officials and their appointees under the terms of the politics-administration separation. How, or if, the seams of the political/career relationship are mended to achieve this is not discussed. The role of Congress in "steering" is also not addressed.[30]

Further, the remnants of patronage remain a key part of contemporary civil service systems. There are two components of modern patronage: the authority of the president (or governor, or mayor) to appoint selected personnel to serve in public organizations, most often in top management or policy positions; and the provisions of the Hatch Act, which, first at the federal level and then at state and local levels as well, prohibited merit employees from participating in political activities, but also protected them from being coerced into doing so by political superiors.

In the federal government, the president retains the right to appoint top-level executives for the cabinet agencies (called PAS appointments, because they are appointed by the president, but must be approved by the Senate), political members of the Senior Executive Service (SES), and a set of positions that are deemed to be "policy sensitive," but are not necessarily top-level management positions, called Schedule C positions. (The president also appoints ambassadors, members of many small commissions, and members of the White House staff, but the relationship of these appointees to the civil service is more indirect.) PAS and SES appointees generally sit at the top of the agencies they are to direct; their purpose is to translate presidential policy initiatives into program outcomes at the agency level. Schedule Cs are generally at lower levels of the organization, often in "special assistant" positions. Most of these appointees are chosen on the basis of partisan affiliation as well as for their management or policy knowledge. By most counts, there are now approximately three thousand appointments available to the president.

Of the appointees, the Schedule Cs are most likely to be appointed for purely political reasons; they are also the fastest-growing group of political appointees. The total number of these appointees doubled in the period from 1976 to 1990. This represents substantially fewer positions than the president could fill immediately after passage of the Pendleton Act, which created the civil service system in 1883. The appointees still make up less than 1 percent of the total federal service; however, even this figure places the United States well above other Western democracies in terms of numbers of patronage appointments. In the British case, for example, there are only about 120 such appointments for the prime minister to make; all other policy and management positions are filled by members of the higher civil service. The number is roughly similar in France; in Germany the number is even smaller, about forty.[31]

The issue of political appointments and patronage has been important in state governments in the United States as well. It has, in fact, been the subject of recent court cases. In Illinois, an effort by Governor James Thompson to gain control of the bureaucracy resulted in "a system [that] was essentially closed to those who had not been politically referred."[32] In *Rutan v. Republican Party of Illinois* (1990), the U.S. Supreme Court ruled that the practices in Illinois infringed on the First Amendment rights of public employees. In doing so, the Court cited and reaffirmed the decisions in *Elrod v. Burns* (1976), also in Illinois, and *Branti v. Finkel* (1980), in New York, in which public employees were dismissed based on their political affiliations. In combination, these cases covered appointment, dismissal, promotion, and transfer actions, and served as a ringing condemnation of patronage except at the top levels of public organizations.[33]

It is also important to note the impact of the Hatch Act and its subsequent revision on members of the public service. The federal Hatch Act was adopted in 1939; its official title was "Act to Prevent Pernicious Political Activities." It was passed at a time of tense relations between the president and the Congress. Many members of Congress, including some from his own party, were concerned at the extent to which merit principles and procedures had been bypassed in some federal agencies during Franklin Roosevelt's presidency. As Peter Benda and David Rosenbloom argue, "The Hatch Act was based on a reasonably coherent concept of what a public service should *not* be."[34] Senator Hatch, the sponsor of the bill, did not want to see a return to the "bad old days" of spoils. In 1940, provisions of the Hatch Act were extended to state and local, as well as federal, employees.

The Hatch Act effectively removed public employees from all political activity except voting and expressing their opinions in a nonpartisan way. The act is discussed in more detail below; it is important here only to note that it placed significant restrictions on public employees as well as on political officials and that it has been consistently challenged in the years since its passage. There were several serious efforts to overturn the provisions of the act (to "un-Hatch" public employees) and in 1993, in the early months of the Clinton administration, Congress passed a bill that removed many of the Hatch Act restrictions. Although previous presidents had vowed to veto such a bill, President Clinton did not. The newly "un-Hatched" federal employees may participate in partisan politics and persuasion; only a limited number of employees in sensitive agencies and occupations such as the Internal Revenue Service and intelligence activities remain covered by political constraints. The long-term implications of this new law are unclear, but are important for the future of the public service and for the concept of merit in public employment.

Effectiveness and Efficiency: The Management Issues

A different, but equally significant, issue for the civil service is the emerging expectation that the system develop and produce excellent managers. This seemingly straightforward objective is tied in important ways to the issues of political direction discussed above. In the American federal system, the chief executives of public organizations are political appointees. Top career managers report directly to them, and it is at this nexus that tensions between political management and the management apparatus created by the merit system can be most acute. If managers are to be "excellent," they will by most definitions also be flexible, innovative, and open to change. They will also have substantial authority, discretion, and individual accountability. The fit between these qualities and those often associated with political responsiveness, particularly the hierarchical model of responsiveness, is not comfortable.

The conflict between traditional civil service systems and the modern concept of management is also problematic. The civil service has neither recruited managers nor emphasized their development. The system generally hires persons with specialized professional or program skills and rewards them for honing those skills. The nature of career development in the federal service reinforces this pattern: many public employees stay with one agency or one program area for a long time, sometimes for their entire careers. This "stovepipe" model of career development—advancing upward within rigidly defined boundaries—creates narrow specialists with in-depth knowledge of limited aspects of the organization. The system does not encourage them to develop the broader perspectives, human-relations skills, or other abilities associated with management. Indeed, most management training in the federal government occurs *after* the employee has assumed her management position, and then only sporadically.

Further, the emphasis on rules and procedures has created an organizational environment in which applying rules and following procedures has been valued more highly than using discretion and flexibility effectively to mobilize resources to achieve organizational objectives. This distinction can be summarized by considering the differences between administration and management. The former describes the neutral civil servant applying the right rule at the right time, but not questioning the rule and certainly not exercising discretion in whether it should be applied. Management, on the other hand, connotes considerable authority, discretion in its use, and accountability for outcomes and product rather than to rules and regulations. Civil service systems generally create administrators, not managers. They do so through a variety of means.

One of the most important is the separation of the personnel function from line management. Managerial authority and prerogatives in recruiting, hiring, and rewarding have been severely constrained by the centralized, standardized personnel function. To the extent that managers are able to exercise flexibility and discretion, it is in manipulating the system into hiring the persons they really wish to hire or promoting the persons they really want to promote. In short, virtually everything about the civil service system and its concomitant rules and regulations works against the development of a strong managerial culture and strong managers.

The wrong incentives are in place and they are in the wrong places. The civil service system was not intended to be a flexible management system; true to its intent, it is not.

As we move into the next century, however, the emphasis on good management in the public service is becoming increasingly central to widely shared perspectives on effective government. How good management is defined, how public managers are recruited and educated, how the relationship between political executives and career civil servants is defined and implemented, and how standards of accountability will operate in a new and more challenging environment will be hotly debated. In 1993, the National Academy of Public Administration noted that "public servants are confronted with a paradox. While the public expects more and better government, workers are burdened with rigid and cumbersome tools that seriously undermine their capacity for efficient and timely action. . . . It is not a question of whether the federal government should change how it manages its human resources. It must change." [35]

Meeting the Challenge of Change

This change will occur in a context that includes dramatic shifts in the kinds of work government does and how it does that work. Growing internationalization and global competition are forcing both public and private organizations to be more effective competitors. Growing deficits and shrinking resources have changed the long-term ability of all organizations to plan and have compelled them to be adaptive and flexible—to do more with less, in many cases. Changing workforce demographics and demands will require the ability to use diversity in constructive and creative ways.

The source for models for the necessary changes that government and civil service systems must undergo is not clear. Certainly for the past one hundred years in the United States and elsewhere the model has been the private sector and the reforms that have originated there. The United States has been unusual in the long-term enthusiasm it has shown for the transfer of techniques and ideas—the notion of running government "like a business" has been around almost as long as government itself in our case—but in the past twenty-five years most modern nations have embraced the transfer when searching for reform. Managerialism, the "effort to transform public administrators into managers who think, act and perform their jobs like private sector managers and run their government organizations like private sector firms," [36] has been a prominent characteristic of government reform in Great Britain, Australia, and New

Zealand. Other Western democracies have also relied on private-sector models for reform design.

The content of the reforms has also been similar: fourteen nations have now borrowed the idea of pay for performance from the private sector and from one another.[37] Reform efforts have been notable for their common emphases on privatization and contracting out, on decentralization, and on creating systems in which members of the higher civil service have more discretion and authority, but also more specific productivity targets. In Australia and New Zealand, those career executives work under the terms of a three- to five-year contract that may be terminated if performance is not satisfactory. Comprehensive reform efforts, such as the Civil Service Reform Act in the United States, the Next Steps initiative in the United Kingdom, and the reforms in Australia and New Zealand have included most of these components in their packages.[38]

Whatever their scope, many previous efforts to change government, the civil service, and public management have amounted to tinkering at the fringes of the system and at the perimeters of the real issues. Reform efforts have also, as B. Guy Peters and Donald Savoie note, generally looked only at the civil service, and not at its political environment, the political institutions that shape it, or the broader role it plays in government. While the reformers may have a vision of government—smaller, less expensive, more flexible—they do not have a vision of the role that public institutions and organizations should play, except that it, too, should be smaller. As a result, Peters and Savoie argue, the reforms made to date could amount to "a sand castle that will crumble when seriously challenged by the first 'political' or 'administrative' crisis, or simply by time."[39]

The real challenge for finding effective models of change and reform for public management and public organizations, therefore, is not in discovering new techniques or approaches to management, nor is it simply in developing better and faster ways of reducing size. It is in laying a realistic foundation for the overarching roles that the civil service and merit play in modern government—deciding what the public service should do—and matching that foundation with sound political support. All the management techniques in the world will falter in the public sector if the environment in which they are implemented is one of distrust and constant challenge. The "intellectual deficit" that now exists in this regard poses what Charles Levine called "the central challenge confronting scholars and public officials in the next decade."[40]

The deficit extends to existing views and conceptions of merit. Merit originally was intended to enhance effective government; it was meant to

ensure competent and meritorious public service. It was to do so by excluding political influence from the daily workings of public organizations. That was in 1883. As we approach a new century, the core purpose
of merit remains important, but the arcane complexity of the current
merit system and the procedural baggage that accompanies its implementation are prime candidates for the public garbage bin. Even as many
parts are discarded, however, the questions "What must be retained?"
and "What is the foundation of merit in a democratic system?" are central; a full understanding of the complex relationship between politics
and merit is more important than ever before.

In the following chapters of this book, the evolution of the merit system is examined, not just to offer a historical perspective, but to illumi-
nate what has been integral to the system in the past—what values have
guided the development of merit, the perception of the role and legitimacy of the public service in governing the United States, and the ever-
thorny issue of the relationship between elected officials and career civil
servants. In the modern world, merit must be about effective problem
solving and management as well as legitimacy and accountability. How
to get there from here is a crucial political and policy issue.

Chapter Two

The Origins

of the

Merit System

The controversy surrounding the American civil service predates the institution itself. It is an important part of constitutional and political history and reflects many of the tensions inherent in the American view of government. The controversy has three major components: the proper limits to the powers of government and governmental institutions; the locus of control over the bureaucracy (the president or the Congress); and the nature and quality of the public service. In some respects, the years preceding the formation of the civil service are more important to an understanding of it than are the years since its formal creation.

It has been argued that the American civil service is extraconstitutional. That is, the founders did not provide for the *administration* of government; the Constitution does not specifically address the administrative function. Rather, by giving the president the executive power to appoint department heads and others, the Constitution implicitly places administration within the executive branch. Francis Rourke notes, however, that, "showing a certain penchant for surprises," the framers inserted other provisions that muddied the issue. "They authorized Congress to establish and empower all the agencies that might thereafter lie within the domain of the White House, along with the right to determine how much financial support each of these organizations would receive." [1] In addition, the Senate was given approval power over top presidential nominees. This bifurcation of control and responsibility, which Rourke refers to as "joint custody" of the bureaucracy,[2] became the subject of a dispute between the president and the Congress that remains to be resolved.

The Constitution's emphasis on the separation of powers and on checks and balances for those powers reflects a distrust of the institutions of state the colonists had experienced under British rule; public bureaucracies fell into that category. On the other hand, the framers of the Constitution—which Philip Kurland has called "a document of the imagination that is treated as if it were real"[3]—could not foresee the size and scope of contemporary government and its institutions, which have created problems of control and accountability far beyond any conceived by the founders.

At least one of the founders did argue, however, that administration should play a positive role in good government. Alexander Hamilton wrote in the *Federalist Papers* that "the true test of a good government is its aptitude and tendency to produce a good administration."[4] Indeed, Hamilton's view that the vitality of the state depended on a strong executive and a central and creative role for administration provided an enduring theme for the debates that swirled around the Constitution and the formation of the new government.

Despite the passion with which Hamilton advanced his view of government and administration, the contemporary public service is best understood by examining the views of those with whom Hamilton debated. In many respects, Thomas Jefferson provided an alternative view of government. He believed that a strong central government and administration would be detrimental to the energy of the state. Jefferson argued strongly for more-limited government and for direct citizen involvement. His time in France provided him not only with a fondness for French ice cream and fine wine, but with a serious distaste for the administrative controls he had observed. Jefferson wanted the new American state to focus on the rights of the individual citizen and viewed any tendency toward centralization and strength in national government as a diminution of citizenship.[5]

With Hamilton and Jefferson anchoring points of the debate regarding the strength of the central government, James Madison emerged somewhere in the middle. His famous passage in Federalist no. 51 aptly summarizes his view of both government and its citizens: "If men were angels," he wrote, "no government would be necessary. . . . In framing a government which is to be administered by men over men, the great difficulty lies in this: you must first enable the government to control the governed; and in the next place oblige it to control itself."[6]

Thus, the debate included a rich diversity of strongly held views about the roles of the central government and of individual citizens, the relationship of citizen to government, and the concentration of power in any level of government or governmental institution. The fear of concentrated power was nearly matched (in everyone except Jefferson) by the fear of rampant citizen self-interest. What arose from the debates was not a clear acclamation of either government or citizen. Rather, the concepts of the separation of powers, checks and balances, and judicial oversight implied a continuing need to search for a fair solution. From this compromise and shaky consensus, tenuous legitimacy, widely diffused power and authority, and a continuing distrust of both government and citizen came the foundations for the growth and development of government and its institutions in the United States.

Why does this matter for the public service? Because, as Woodrow Wilson noted, it is more difficult to run a constitution than to frame one.[7] The unresolved conflicts that had been papered over by compromise in the Constitution emerged intact in the new government. As political and governmental institutions evolved, the old issues became central. The public service—its legitimacy, its accountability, its characteristics, its quality, and its size—assumed an early significance.

The Early Public Service

Frederick Mosher refers to the period from 1789 to 1829 as "Government by Gentlemen."[8] During that time, presidents operated with what Mosher terms "surprisingly little guidance" from the Constitution in building the foundation of the public service. There is consensus among historians that George Washington established a positive precedent in emphasizing competence and fitness of character, rather than personal ties or nepotism. It is important to note, however, that the pool of persons from which Washington chose his appointments was small, homogeneous, and elite. Although the new American republic strongly advocated egalitarianism, the large landowners and wealthy merchants who had been most active in articulating the goals and ideals of the new government were also its first elected representatives, judges, and public servants. In choosing members of this group as the first appointed public servants, Washington chose men like himself, who considered public service an honor, indeed, perhaps a duty.[9] There is some evidence that Washington gave preference to those who had been successful state officeholders and to those who had supported the ratification of the Constitution.[10]

At this early level of governmental development, federal public servants were of two types: the high-ranking officials appointed by the president to what would now be termed executive and policy positions, and the workers, such as clerks and accountants, who actually delivered or monitored government services and who were generally located in field offices outside Washington.[11] It was the high-ranking officials who were drawn largely from the elite; the workers were more representative of the citizenry in general. The "stable"[12] public service of the Federalist era, while setting a standard for effective and competent public service, also experienced in microcosm problems that would later become broader issues. The most significant of these was the replacement of the appointive officers after the election of a new president. The issue of the representativeness of the public service also began to emerge.

The presidency of Thomas Jefferson was notable in several respects. First, his election marked a partisan shift, replacing Federalists with Republicans. Jefferson articulated the first argument for patronage in the system when he contended that a limited number of offices ought to be divided between the parties and that party service was a valid criterion for appointment to the public service. Following his own counsel, President Jefferson did, in fact, remove appointees for partisan reasons. He wrote to a friend in 1801, "I had foreseen, years ago, that the first republican president who should come into office after all the places in government had become exclusively occupied by federalists would have a dreadful operation to perform. That the republicans would consent to a continuation of everything in federalist hands was not to be expected, because it was neither just nor politic. On him, then, was to devolve the office of an executioner, that of lopping off."[13]

Second, Jefferson questioned the representativeness of the public service and argued that it should more accurately reflect the citizenry. At the same time, he argued against the growth of government and worried about its quality.

Inevitably, however, that growth occurred. Paul Van Riper notes that federal employment grew from three thousand in 1800 to six thousand in 1816. By 1831 the number had reached twenty thousand.[14] The president continued to enjoy essentially unlimited power to appoint and remove top-level employees; in 1820 Congress passed the "Four Years Law," which limited the terms of many public offices and allowed for removal for cause. The law was intended to constrain the power of the president, but in practice it assured both turnover and opportunities for new appointments. Presidents used their appointment and removal powers liberally. President John Adams made original appointments to over two-thirds of the positions available to him, President Jefferson made seventy-three of ninety-two possible appointments, and President Madison and President Monroe followed the pattern.[15]

In contrast, the lower levels of the public organizations remained rather stable and gave rise to another kind of concern. The growth of public employment and the lack of an effective system of controls allowed some abuses of office. Carl Fish notes that public employees remained in office despite extended illnesses, that offices were not reviewed to determine whether they continued to be necessary, and that internal promotions and appointments of friends, and sometimes family, to vacant positions evoked criticism. The early goals of the Federalists for high standards of competence and integrity in the public service, while essentially intact in the early nineteenth century, had become somewhat tarnished. The public service was perceived to be tied too closely to the aristocracy, a perception not diminished by the views of some of the early presidents. Despite his concern for a government that was more representative, for example, in 1813 Jefferson wrote to John Adams: "I agree with you that there is a natural aristocracy among men. The grounds of this are virtue and talents . . . may we not even say, that the form of government is best which provides the most effectually for a pure selection of these natural aristoi into the offices of government?"[16]

Members of Congress, responding to demands for greater democracy in the public service, as well as their own wishes to have a greater voice in the process, increased their efforts to control the president's power of appointment. In 1826 a committee chaired by Senator Thomas Benton proposed senatorial confirmation of more positions and recommended that the president submit to Congress in writing his reasons for removal of presidential appointees. Senator Benton observed that "the exercise of great patronage in the hands of one man has a constant tendency to sully the purity of our institutions, and to endanger the liberties of the country. This doctrine is not new. A jealousy of power, and of the influence of patronage which must always accompany its exercise, has ever been a distinguished feature of the American character."[17]

Thus, in the first thirty years of the history of the civil service, many of the tensions inherent in the institutions created by the Constitution had become visible. The power of the civil service itself remained incipient. The power to control it, however, was becoming important. The struggle between the president and the Congress in that regard was already apparent. The nature and quality of the institution was also attracting new attention. Landowners, merchants, and wealthy professionals were not representative of the population of the United States. Presidential arguments for a "natural aristocracy" based on talent and virtue did not translate into a public service that was accessible to the "common man." The election of Andrew Jackson by those common men in 1828 brought the tensions into politics and into the civil service itself.

Government of the People

The next major development in the history of the American public service is often referred to as the "Spoils Era." In that time, patronage became central to public employment, although it had been of some concern since the presidency of Thomas Jefferson. Andrew Jackson established no precedents in his use of presidential appointment and removal power; he made approximately the same number of new appointments as had Jefferson twenty years earlier. Further, the Jackson appointees were not dramatically different from those of earlier presidents; although he did appoint more from what Mosher terms "middle-ranking occupations," [18] these men were outnumbered by his elite appointees. President Jackson did, however, begin systematically to challenge some of the practices that had become established in the still-young public service. He also began to enlarge the role of political loyalty in the selection process. Of equal significance, Jackson chose the occasion of his first annual message in 1829 to articulate his "doctrine of the simplicity of public work." [19] In that address, Jackson stated that

> There are, perhaps, few men who can for any great length of time enjoy office and power without being more or less under the influence of feelings unfavorable to the faithful discharge of their public duties. . . . The duties of all public offices are, or at least admit of being made, so plain and simple that men of intelligence may readily qualify themselves for their performance; and all can not but believe that more is lost by the long continuance of men in office than is generally gained by their experience.

This is Jackson's major contribution to the shaping of the public service, and it is far removed from Jefferson's concept of a natural aristocracy destined to serve: there is nothing special about public service, and simple qualifications—intelligence and common sense—are adequate to carry out its duties.

This view of government was strengthened by the growth in mass political participation and the emergence of organized political parties. Jackson used patronage to strengthen his own party; he also used it as a bargaining chip with Congress to gain its acquiescence in his programs. Outside Washington, urban political machines began to grow. Patronage was fundamental to their strength. In 1835, Jackson made that same link for the president and the party that elected him: "It is certain that whichever party makes the President, must give direction to this administration. . . . No one can carry on this Government without support, and the Head of it must rely for support on the party by whose suffrages he is elected." [20]

The marriage of mass politics and public employment was happier for politics than for the public service. At the federal, state, and local levels of government, patronage took firm root in the mid-1800s. With it came the substitution of partisan loyalty for essentially all other qualifications for public office. In addition, a link between federal employment and faithfulness and service to local machines was created. Leonard White notes that after 1829, federal employees were subject to local party requirements such as "obligations to pay party assessments, to do party work at election time, and to 'vote right' " as a condition of continued employment.[21]

If Andrew Jackson had been relatively restrained in his appointment and removal activities (Fish observes that Jackson made 252 new appointments out of a possible 612),[22] presidents that followed were more active. When the Whigs were victorious in 1840, they expanded Jackson's practices (despite having condemned them in the campaign), and public jobs were openly bought and sold. There was one important change during this time, however. Although he served only four weeks of his presidential term before his death, William Henry Harrison was successful in ordering that federal employees be prohibited from engaging in political activity.

Overall, the spoils system was at its most rampant in the period from 1845 to 1865. After his election in 1844, President James Polk promised to remove dishonest employees, but did not state his intentions regarding those who had performed well. In the end, he removed more employees than any of the presidents who preceded him. At the inauguration of Zachary Taylor four years later, William Seward wrote that "the world seems almost divided into two classes: those who are going to California in search of gold, and those going to Washington in quest of office." [23] In Taylor's administration, a third of all government employees resigned or were removed from office. What Henry Clay had earlier termed a "detestable system" was firmly entrenched not only for civilian jobs, but for many military jobs as well. President James Buchanan, at a time of increasing national turmoil, removed not only members of the opposing party but members of his own party who had not supported him. Buchanan also voiced support for complete rotation of federal positions every four years. The Civil Service Commission later characterized this as the "most extreme statement on spoils ever made in the United States." [24]

Abraham Lincoln also employed patronage extensively, even though he deplored the demands it made on the president and the damage it did to the quality of public employment. Carl Fish estimates that Lincoln removed 1,457 incumbents from the 1,639 positions available to him; the president was under constant pressure from job seekers.[25] At one point, observing the hundreds of office seekers on the White House grounds, Lincoln said, "There you see something which will, in the course of time, become a greater danger to the republic than the rebellion itself."[26]

The Civil War provided tragic evidence of the impact of spoils on the quality of public employees. Unqualified civilians had been given higher ranks than longtime members of the military, and the Union army's early performance reflected this lack of experience and understanding of military discipline. Although it became a topic of jokes (one satirist attributed the Union defeat at Bull Run to the announcement of three vacancies at the New York customhouse),[27] the effectiveness of the Union army and of the federal government in the Civil War was undermined by the spoils system.

Spoils exacerbated other national tragedies as well. Leonard White cites the report of the 1868 Indian Peace Commission: "The records are abundant to show that (federal) agents have pocketed the funds appropriated by the government and driven the Indians to starvation. . . . For a long time these officers have been selected from partisan ranks, not so much on account of honesty and qualification as for devotion to party interest and their willingness to apply the money of the Indians to promote the selfish schemes of local politicians."[28]

After Lincoln's assassination, Andrew Johnson used patronage to strengthen his own position and to coax congressional cooperation in the early years of Reconstruction. In 1867, Congress, concerned about the extent of spoils and its own lack of control, passed the Tenure of Office Act. The act required Senate approval for *removal* from office. President Johnson believed it to be unconstitutional and, to prove his point, removed the secretary of war from his post. Congress began impeachment proceedings and failed by only one vote to remove Johnson.

Both the president and the Congress had profited from spoils; members of Congress had pursued patronage appointments for their supporters with considerable vigor and had come to view some appointments as a privilege of office. Nonetheless, the excesses and the costs of spoils were becoming impossible to ignore. As Frederick Mosher notes, "The egalitarian drive which spurred and rationalized the spoils system proved decreasingly effective as a guarantor of popular direction and control of administration. . . . the new criteria for appointment produced administrators little more representative of the whole people than before . . . and made more effectively possible . . . decision-making behind the scenes—invisible government, as it was called." [29]

Congress created the Joint Select Committee on Retrenchment, one of whose tasks was to consider the use of examinations for entry to federal employment. The committee's report was issued in 1868; it was a ringing condemnation of spoils. The alternative the report proposed was modeled on the British civil service system. Elements of the systems in China, Prussia, and France were also discussed. The recommendations made in the report were not adopted; they served an important purpose, however, in that they built on modest reforms already in place and provided a foundation for more comprehensive efforts.

The State of the Public Service before the Pendleton Act

Despite the overwhelming impact of spoils, some limited reforms had occurred in the period from 1830 to the end of the Civil War. White argues that by 1850 a "dual system" [30] had emerged in the public service: the career service and the spoils system. The career service, he notes, could be found in such scientific and professional agencies as the Coast Survey, the Naval Observatory, the Navy Medical Corps, and the Smithsonian Institution. The army had created examinations for its surgeons and the cadets at West Point as early as 1814.

In 1853, Congress passed legislation that provided for examinations for clerks in Washington (primarily in the post office and the General Land Office) and for a rudimentary classification system. It is important to note that those taking the examinations had to be recommended by the secretary of the department; still, the reintroduction of the idea of necessary skills as qualifications was a departure from the predominant qualification of partisan loyalty. In addition, the equation of tenure with development of skills and expertise again became a part of the discussion.

Carl Fish points to two flaws in the reforms adopted prior to 1860. First, he says, "they aimed rather to hinder removals than to control appointments, and secondly, they tended to shift the power from the shoulders of the president to the Senate, and by dividing the burden to do away with all sense of personal responsibility." [31] Reforms after the Civil War focused more on fundamental changes in the character of the public service and on entry into it. Patronage was now so well entrenched, however, that reform efforts faced enormous opposition. Good intentions were a poor match for political power.

The administration of Ulysses S. Grant provides ample testimony. Grant himself ran on a reform platform; by the time of his inauguration he had backed away from civil service reform as an objective of his presidency. Two of his appointees, at the Departments of the Interior and Treasury, did institute competitive examinations for their departments. Jacob Cox, at the Department of the Interior, introduced a merit system there in July 1870. In November 1870, he resigned under pressure from members of Congress looking for patronage appointments in his department.[32] Grant himself had a somewhat spotty record on reform that clearly reflected the pressures of spoils on reformers and politicians alike. His tenure in office was marked by corruption in the highest offices; early in his first term, on the other hand, he began once again to pursue civil service reform. In his second annual message he said that "the present system does not secure the best men, and often not even fit men, for public place."[33]

In 1871, a rider attached to an appropriations bill authorized the president to "prescribe such regulations for the admission of persons into the civil service of the United States as may best promote the efficiency thereof, and to ascertain the fitness of each candidate in respect to age, health, character, knowledge, and ability."[34] This legislation marked the beginning of a formal merit system in the United States; given the battles between the president and the Congress over appointment and removal power to this point in history, it is notable that the legislation gave to the president the power to direct and appoint the civil service.

Under the terms of the law, President Grant created the Advisory Board for the Civil Service; the group was later called the Civil Service Commission. It had seven members. The first chair was George William Curtis, who would become a leading advocate for broader civil service reform. The commission lived for only two years; in 1873, Congress did not fund it. Competitive examinations continued for two more years, but, because of the lack of funding, Grant discontinued them in 1875.

The brief experiment did lay the groundwork for the eventual creation of a permanent merit system. Of equal importance, it demonstrated the tenacious attractiveness of spoils. Members of Congress viewed continuation of patronage as central to their own stability in office. The president was under constant pressure from members of his own party to enlarge, not constrict, the practice. Further, the experiment with the Civil Service Commission clarified the potential power shift if full authority for the civil service rested in the executive office of the president. This issue would reemerge, cast in constitutional terms, in future reform efforts.

Other issues and guidelines would also arise from this abbreviated effort. Many characteristics of the contemporary civil service had their origin in this early commission; many contemporary problems were first addressed there. One of the most notable is the "rule of three," which states that the appointing officer must choose one of the top three scorers on the civil service examination list, and cannot choose from the entire list. This rule was initially adopted to bypass what was considered a constitutional prohibition on limiting the appointment power of department heads.[35] A second major and enduring issue is that of preferential treatment for military veterans in admission to the civil service. It was proposed that veterans of the Civil War be given special consideration in admission. The first commission rejected this idea; later commissions did not. The interactive effects of these two early decisions shaped, and continue to shape, the United States civil service in profound ways.

The nature and tone of the campaign for civil service reform at this period in history is significant. A century after the first major reform, the civil service is most often discussed in disparaging terms. It is viewed as bland and colorless, filled with faceless, anonymous bureaucrats in equally anonymous bureaucracies. In the late 1800s, however, the debate was passionate and moralistic; it was about political power and its abuse and about the quality of government. Civil service systems, or merit systems, were equated with "good" government. They represented fair and equitable examinations, qualified public servants, and a commitment to the higher ideals of the state. Politics, on the other hand, had come to represent what was wrong with government. The early reformers believed deeply that if civil service systems were to function properly, the influence of politics and politicians would have to be completely removed from them. Mosher writes, "Few reform movements in American history could draw so clear a distinction between right and wrong, between the 'good guys' and the 'bad guys.' "[36] At the same time, the intricate connection between politics and merit was clearly recognized: political excess had created the problem, but until politicians themselves rejected that excess, no solution would be found.

The Pendleton Act and the Merit System

Both the scope and the nature of the pressure for reform changed in the years immediately preceding passage of the Pendleton Act. Rutherford B. Hayes, elected in 1876, was committed to reform despite his shaky electoral base. The number of state and local reform leagues was growing, and civil service reform was emerging as an issue in congressional elections. Hayes used his executive authority to extend examinations whenever possible; his appointee at the Department of the Interior was Carl Schurz, a prominent and vocal reformer. Schurz reinstated the examination system that had been created for that department in 1871. At the election of James Garfield in 1880, there was, if not overwhelming pressure for reform, at least growing support. The Civil Service Commission summarized the climate for reform in these terms: "Garfield . . . was inaugurated at a time when, although the spoils system was still in massive use, the executive branch was pushing moderately hard for civil service reform, public opinion was moderately favorable toward it, and the Congress was moderately, rather than violently, opposing it."[37]

As is often the case in American public policy, however, it was a dramatic event that was the catalyst for action. President Garfield, like all presidents in the fifty years before him, was the target of aggressive job seekers. He noted in his journal, "My day is frittered away by the personal seeking of people, when it ought to be given over to the great problems which concern the whole country. Four years of this kind of intellectual dissipation may cripple me for the rest of my life."[38]

President Garfield was not to be so lucky. A former campaign worker, believing he deserved to be appointed U.S. consul in Paris, had harassed Garfield incessantly in the days after the election. In July, as the president waited to board a train, that office seeker shot him. Garfield died ten weeks later. A leading national magazine editorialized: "This dire calamity is part of the penalty we pay for permitting a practice for which as a public benefit not a solitary word can be urged, and which, while stimulating the deadliest passions, degrades our politics and corrupts our national character. The spoils system is a vast public evil."[39]

One month after Garfield's death, the National Civil Service Reform League was founded. Reform at the national level was its top priority. At the end of 1881, a reform bill that had been drafted by Dorman Eaton was introduced by Senator Pendleton of Ohio, the chair of the Senate Committee on Civil Service Reform. Eaton had earlier reported to President Hayes on the British civil service system. There had also been earlier correspondence with the British reformers Sir Stafford Northcote and Sir Charles Trevelyan, whose report on the British system led to changes there. While the proposed American system was modeled on the British one, however, it was not an exact replica, and debate in the Senate produced revisions that were uniquely American in their emphasis. At the heart of the legislation was one fundamental merit principle: admission to the civil service would be only through fair, open, and competitive examinations.

Provisions of the act in the form in which it passed included an emphasis on practical skills and knowledge in the examinations, rather than the British emphasis on academic credentials and knowledge. The act also rejected the British practice of permitting entry only at the lowest grades, and allowed open competition in promotional as well as entry examinations. These provisions were seen as reflecting the American values of equality and fairness. The decreased emphasis on formal education encouraged a focus on independence and common sense, qualities considered more American than European.

The legislation addressed the constitutional issue about placing the Civil Service Commission under presidential control and permitting the president to delegate authority to it. The act did not allow the commission to make appointments, but instead only let it recommend the three best-qualified applicants for each position—which represents the reemergence of the "rule of three." The president's removal power was not addressed; the reformers reasoned that "there would be no temptation to remove employees for political reasons if the replacements could not be selected politically." [40] The Civil Service Commission was to have three members, appointed by the president and confirmed by the Senate. The legislation provided that 10 percent of the existing federal workforce would be covered by the merit system; the president was given the authority to include additional members by executive order. The bill was signed by President Chester A. Arthur in January 1883. It had passed with bipartisan support, but with a sizable portion of members of both houses absent.

Conclusion

Clearly, the Pendleton Act was important legislation, and it has had a lasting impact on the public service in the United States. On the other hand, many of its features, however reasonable or necessary they seemed at the time, contributed to a public personnel system that is currently dysfunctional in many ways. Three examples illustrate this point.

1. The initial coverage of only 10 percent of the workforce has been characterized by Paul Van Riper in the following way: "If the act permitted an orderly retreat of parties from their prerogatives of plunder, it made possible as well the gradual administrative development of the merit system." [41] It may be true that the act permitted "orderly retreat"; it is equally true that the 10 percent limit was a classically political solution to a difficult problem. The provisions of the Pendleton Act, intending to separate politics and merit, made the expansion of merit

nearly totally dependent on the political will of the president. Merit would proceed only if politics permitted it to do so. This ensured that development would not be orderly or necessarily coherent. In the American policy tradition, it would be incremental and gradual, addressing one limited issue or problem at a time.

In addition, the legislation did not create a higher civil service or an administrative class, as did the British model. The elite nature of such a group was deemed incompatible with the American emphasis on the common person and on equality; further, it raised the issue of educational requirements, which had already been dismissed in the testing decisions. The practical implication of this decision was to leave the top policy positions in each agency to patronage, because merit system employees were to be neutral in such matters. This practice, which will be discussed in more detail below, was fundamental to the creation of organizations in the federal government that are notable for being staffed by a stable group of career civil servants, but directed by a much smaller group of patronage appointees serving both a policy and an executive function, who depart with every election (and often more frequently). The ability of this small group to direct the career service effectively has been a concern of every president since the New Deal.

2. The emphasis on the practical nature of the entrance examinations carried with it the implication that there was nothing very different or difficult about most federal jobs—a carryover from Jackson's "simplicity of public work" principle. Further, the commitment to equal treatment for all job applicants and members of the civil service led to an early and quickly expanding reliance on centralized standardization. In combination, these emphases led to the need for some system to organize, or classify, federal jobs. Because the examinations did not differentiate between qualifications and necessary skills, the classification systems had to do so in detailed and precise terms. This has led to the development of a narrow and rigid classification system, which has been cited as a problem for most of this century.

3. Finally, the creation of the Civil Service Commission established the practice of removing the personnel function from general management activities. As Mosher notes, the Civil Service Commission quickly became "an offsetting power unto itself against political pressures from the parties, the Congress, the President, and other units in the administration. It became not alone an instrument for the orderly administration of a merit system, but a watchdog against possible transgressions against such a system." [42]

In the interests of protecting merit from politics, the commission and its successors began to develop an elaborate set of rules and regulations that served to insulate members of the civil service not only from politics and political abuse, but from the career managers who were responsible for supervising their daily activities. As the merit system developed and the rules became more extensive, the separation of personnel administration from management became a hallmark of the American civil service system. As time has shown, however, it has also become one of the system's most vexing problems.

Even at this early stage of its development, then, the civil service had both the essential characteristics of today's system and the seeds of its current problems. The constitutional silence on the role of administration, the fear of presidential abuse of removal and appointment authority, the commitment of both Congress and the White House to patronage, and the emerging recognition of the power that the civil service could wield were important formative influences. The limited nature of the first merit system was also significant. So, too, was the strongly moral tone of the reform and the accompanying belief that "good" government could be achieved only by insulating the civil service from undue influence, from whatever source. All these issues continue to be relevant. An examination of the critical events in the development of the system and their impact on its overall effectiveness is useful in understanding both the strengths and the weaknesses of the contemporary civil service. That is the intent of the next chapter.

Chapter Three

The Evolution

of the

Merit System

Although the Pendleton Act is often credited with creating the federal merit system, the limited coverage of the act ensured that it would be only one of many influences on the civil service. Indeed, many of the most ardent advocates of reform had argued that the growth of merit *must* be gradual and achieved through what Dorman Eaton termed "educational influence" and "public enlightenment." In his tract detailing the civil service system in Great Britain, he wrote: "There is no greater delusion than the theory held by some worthy but inexperienced and sanguine reformers who, scorning deliberate and educational processes, expect the removal of all our abuses to be brought about, suddenly, in a grand reform campaign, which shall drive all bad men from office and inaugurate an era of purity and patriotism." [1]

The first years after the act's implementation revealed the difficulties of this approach; they provide classic evidence of the effect of shifting political values and priorities on the incremental and incoherent development of policy. Equally significantly, they demonstrate the tenuous link between the merit system and good government in the minds of many elected officials. Government by merit quickly became entangled in political reality; the foundation of merit was redefined by these political encounters. For the key events that shaped the foundation during this period, see table 3.1.

Table 3.1   Expansion of the Merit System during Early Presidential Terms

President	Term	Event
Chester Arthur	1881–1885	Through the Pendleton Act of 1883, created the merit system
Grover Cleveland	1885–1889	Extended the competitive civil service in 1888 by 5,320 positions through blanketing in the Railway Mail Service
Benjamin Harrison	1889–1893	Extended the competitive civil service by blanketing in the Indian Service, Fish Commission, and Weather Bureau
Grover Cleveland	1893–1897	Increased the size of the competitive civil service by 32,000 positions with one order in 1896
William McKinley	1897–1902	Revised the civil service rules in 1899, which excepted over 5,000 positions from the competitive civil service
Theodore Roosevelt	1902–1909	Showed strong support for the civil service reform movement after serving as Civil Service Commissioner from 1889 to 1895
William Taft	1909–1913	Extended the competitive civil service by 39,000 positions by blanketing in fourth-class postmasterships and assistant postmasters and clerks
Woodrow Wilson	1913–1921	Almost doubled the federal workforce to a total of nearly 1,000,000 during World War I
Warren Harding	1921–1923	Saw the competitive civil service hold during the postwar reductions the ground that it had previously gained
Calvin Coolidge	1923–1929	Extended the competitive civil service in 1927 by blanketing in the Bureau of Prohibition
Herbert Hoover	1929–1933	Placed 13,000 previously excepted positions in the competitive civil service
Franklin Roosevelt	1933–1945	Established new temporary emergency agencies, with the majority excepted from the competitive civil service during the Great Depression

Table 3.1   *Continued*

President	Term	Event
		Saw the Ramspeck Act of 1940 extend the competitive civil service to more than 182,000 permanent positions
		Increased the number of federal employees during World War II to 3,816,300 in 1945
Harry Truman	1945–1953	Alternately expanded and contracted the federal workforce, which challenged personnel management
Dwight Eisenhower	1953–1961	Through an executive order in 1953, created a new Schedule C class of positions excepted from the competitive civil service

Source: Data from U.S. Civil Service Commission, *Biography of an Ideal: The Diamond Anniversary History of the Federal Civil Service* (Washington, D.C.: U.S. Government Printing Office, 1958).

The Early Development of the Merit System

The first Civil Service Commission assumed its duties in March 1883; its chair was Dorman Eaton. The commission's first task was to draft the rules and regulations that would govern the civil service system when it became effective three months later. The new system covered about 14,000 employees, of a total of 132,800.[2] The commission was initially staffed by three employees.

Under the first set of rules, the competitive civil service was divided into three parts: the departmental service in Washington, the postal service, and the customs service. Examining boards were created across the country. As the Civil Service Commission notes, these boards were authorized by the commission "to run the competitive examining program, or a part of this program, for an agency installation or a group of installations."[3] This extensive decentralization did not last long; frustrated by the low quality of those being appointed to examining boards by the agencies (and, some would argue, motivated by the elitist inclinations of many of the reformers), the Civil Service Commission soon moved to hire its own staff to carry out the examining function.

Actual hiring under the new system was slow. By September 1883, only two employees had been hired under competitive procedures. One of these employees was a woman, Mary F. Hoyt, who became a clerk in the Treasury Department. The Civil Service Commission did not open all examinations to women, however, until 1919.

In contrast, the unprotected service continued to respond to the pressures for patronage from both the president and the Congress. Grover Cleveland, who as governor of New York had signed the first state civil service law in 1883, was elected to the presidency in 1884. He was a strong supporter of the principle of merit, but came to office after twenty-four years of Republican power. The pressure to make patronage appointments for his own party was strong; Cleveland responded by dismissing large numbers of excepted employees. He also dismissed some employees covered by the new merit system. When he was defeated in his reelection bid, however, he used the power given him by the Pendleton Act to expand the competitive service. He "blanketed in" to the competitive civil service all the employees (in 5,320 positions) in the Railway Mail Service.[4] This addition increased the total size of the competitive service by a third.[5]

The practice of extensive use of patronage removals and appointments, followed by the blanketing in of entire agencies and services at the end of the presidential term, was common. It also served what Michael Nelson terms "the purest of partisan motives," for all those added to the merit system were previous appointees of the president.[6] Benjamin Harrison blanketed in another three agencies during his term; this time the Indian Service, one of the most corrupt agencies under spoils, was included.

In Cleveland's second term, beginning in 1893, he pursued merit more actively, creating a single set of civil service rules to replace the myriad that existed in each agency and extending the competitive service by more than thirty thousand. This meant that the number of spoils appointments available to members of Congress and to succeeding presidents was significantly diminished.

The problems thus posed for presidents became clear in the next term. McKinley vacillated on the merit system; he revised civil service rules to remove about five thousand positions from the competitive service and return them to patronage, and allowed significant numbers of political appointments to be converted to classified appointments. Nonetheless, by 1900 more than 40 percent of the total civil service was classified. This gradual growth continued to the time of the New Deal; it resumed again at the beginning of World War II (see fig. 3.1).

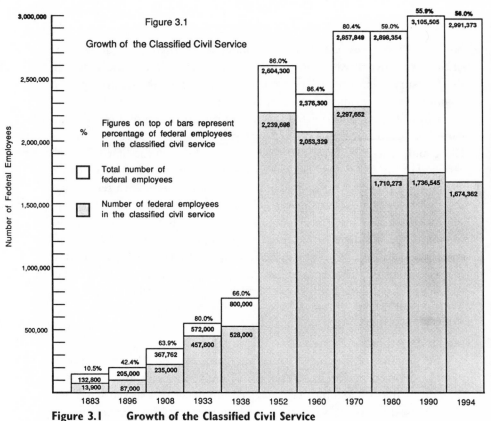

Figure 3.1   Growth of the Classified Civil Service
Sources: U.S. Civil Service Commission, *Biography of an Ideal: The Diamond Anniversary History of the Federal Civil Service* (Washington, D.C.: U.S. Government Printing Office, 1958), and Office of Workforce Information, U.S. Office of Personnel Management.

A Neutral Civil Service?

The early period in the history of the civil service was a time of strongly moralistic advocacy of merit. There was a clear moral tone, even a passion, among the reformers who urged that the spoils system be abandoned. A disdain for politics was evident; there was also considerable elitism on the part of the reformers. They were rejecting "government by the common man," which had led, in their view, to the excesses of spoils. To some extent, this necessitated rejecting the "common man" as well. Theodore Roosevelt, appointed to the Civil Service Commission in 1889, observed that "the civil service reform movement was one from above downwards, and the men who took the lead in it were not men who as a rule possessed a very profound sympathy with or understanding of the ways of thought and life of their average fellow citizen." [7] President Cleveland concurred, calling the reformers "supercilious" and "self-righteous," noting they demanded "complete and immediate perfection." [8]

The loftiness of the reform movement's ideals and objectives added to the problems of the new system. If merit was "good" and politics and spoils unfailingly "bad," how were members of the classified service to operate in a profoundly political environment? How could elected officials provide direction, but avoid abuse? How, in fact, could political direction set the proper objectives for good government if politics itself was so flawed?

The early years of the civil service system's development saw continuous turmoil, as small numbers of members of the classified service worked with much larger numbers of patronage appointees. Further, because the Pendleton Act had not created an administrative class (a higher civil service such as that found in Great Britain), policy direction had to come from the president or from political appointees. These appointees and members of the classified service were somehow to work together, in the same organization, for the same goals.

Frederick Mosher calls the early solution to this dilemma (a solution that would continue to be used over the years) a crutch, rather than a real solution. The doctrine of the separation of politics and administration—what has come to be called the "politics-administration dichotomy"—was advanced shortly after the passage of the Pendleton Act, initially in the writings of Woodrow Wilson, and later by Frank Goodnow and others.[9] Wilson articulated the concept in these terms:

> Seeing clearly every day new things which the state ought to do, the next thing is to see clearly how it ought to do them. This is why there should be a science of administration which shall seek to straighten the paths of government, to make its business less unbusinesslike, to strengthen and purify its administration, and to crown its duties with dutifulness. . . . The field of administration is a field of business. It is removed from the hurry and strife of politics; it at most points stands apart even from the debatable ground of constitutional study. It is a part of political life only as the methods of the counting-house are a part of the life of society; only as machinery is part of the manufactured product.[10]

Wilson's argument that administrative questions are not political questions was fundamental to the creation of both a neutral civil service and a paradigm of public administration in which administrative processes could be viewed as regularized, predictable, and even scientific. It was central to the development of what came to be known as the science of administration in the United States. It also anticipated a major shift from the values of "good government" and morality that had marked initial reform efforts to more neutral values associated with efficiency, standardization, and reduced cost. Equally important for the modern public service, the argument for separating politics from administration—whether or not one advocated a complete dichotomy—returned to the issues of constitutional legitimacy that had been discussed earlier. In contending that administration was not political, but could be perfectly responsive to political (but primarily presidential) direction, Wilson set the parameters for the modern debate about the relationships between the president and the bureaucracy and between the president and the Congress in administrative matters.

Science and Efficiency

The development of the civil service in the period from the early 1900s to about 1930 was marked by three general principles: (1) government work was no different from any other; it could be regularized, measured, and easily understood by its political directors; (2) because the work was simple and predictable, it could be engineered to achieve greater, and perhaps maximum, efficiency; and (3) the model for achieving greater efficiency and effectiveness in the public sector was provided by private-sector corporations. Because much of the work of corporations at that time consisted of routine, assembly-line tasks, it was assumed that government work was similar. The impact of these principles was enormous and continues to the present day.

The early application of these principles to government coincided with the presidency of Theodore Roosevelt. Roosevelt had been a member of the Civil Service Commission for six years before he became president. He had a keen understanding of both the strengths and the weaknesses of the system. Further, because Roosevelt succeeded a Republican president, he did not encounter the pressures for patronage common to the transition from one party to another. President Roosevelt expanded competitive civil service coverage and emphasized the constraints on political activity for members of that service. During his presidency the total number of classified employees surpassed the total number of patronage employees for the first time. He also began efforts to streamline the administration of the civil service, primarily in relation to the examining function.

Roosevelt was responsible for convening the first meeting of states and cities with civil service systems; this meeting was a milestone in emphasizing personnel administration rather than good government, which had been the focus of earlier reformers. The shift to a personnel focus was important for two reasons: first, it defined good government and the role of the civil service in it as the application of standardized rules and procedures to government activities. This was a clear move away from the more insular emphasis of the earlier years. Second, the door was opened for the actual application of the ideas of theorists such as Wilson and Goodnow.

The Roosevelt years saw the reemergence of the strength of the president in directing administration. Peri Arnold observes that, in appointing the Keep Commission to examine government operations in 1905 and in urging more "businesslike" practices on government, Roosevelt "assumed that the president ought to be responsible for the condition of administration and that he could plan and effect administrative reforms. The governmental context of national administration was turning upside down from its 19th century condition." [11]

That "condition" had placed primary responsibility for reform and administration with Congress. Congress had appointed two commissions to examine issues related to government organization and operations in the late 1800s. Ronald Moe notes that "neither inquiry discussed the presidential office or what role that office might be expected to play in the improvement of the conduct of the executive branch." [12]

The significance of this shift should not be underestimated. It marked a new stage in the debate between Congress and the executive about direction of the bureaucracy. More subtly, it began the pendulum's swing back toward the legitimacy of politics and political involvement in the civil service. The "evil influence" identified by the early reformers was being transformed into something more positive. In combination with the new emphasis on neutral personnel administration, this shift supported the redefinition of merit from a moral force to something that was much more mundane and technical in nature.

This is not to suggest that the patronage system had somehow been purified. Woodrow Wilson, who was a strong advocate of reform in the civil service and who had been active in the National Civil Service Reform Association prior to his election as president, felt plagued by the continuing impact of patronage. He wrote, "The matter of patronage is a thorny path that daily makes me wish I had never been born." [13]

Nonetheless, the move toward economy, efficiency, and greater centralization in the executive office of the president continued throughout the next two decades. William Howard Taft appointed the Taft Commission on Economy and Efficiency in 1910. That commission recommended the creation of a central Bureau of the Budget (responsible to the president) and, significantly for the civil service, a Bureau of Efficiency within the Civil Service Commission. The Bureau of Efficiency was created in 1916; the Bureau of the Budget followed in 1921. These institutions marked the high point of the economy-and-efficiency movement and of the impact of scientific management on government.

Administration as Science

"Scientific management," or "administration as science," was a set of academic theories that sought to apply scientific and business principles to the practice of public administration. Woodrow Wilson and Frank Goodnow contributed to this movement, as did such theorists as Frederick Taylor and Luther Gulick. Advocates of scientific management argued that, given the simple and routine nature of much government work, principles could be discovered that described the one best and most efficient way to perform each major task. The principles could be applied across organizations government wide, and would permit rigorous analysis of the extent to which each employee and unit performed efficiently. Neutrality and objectivity in the receipt of direction and performance of tasks were critical to efficiency.

The approach was summarized succinctly by General Charles Dawes, the first director of the Bureau of the Budget, who described the function of the bureau in his first report to the Congress:

> We in the Bureau of the Budget are not concerned with matters of policy. The President . . . and Congress determine the great questions of policy. As for us, we are men down in the stokehole of the ship of state, and we are concerned simply with the economical handling of fuel. The President and Congress determine which way the ship sails, for that is a matter of policy, but we in the hold of the ship have something to do with how far she can sail through the way in which, in our humbler place, we apply common sense business principles. . . . Again I say we have nothing to do with policy. Much as we love the President, if Congress, in its omnipotence over appropriations and in accordance with its authority over policy, passed a law that garbage should be put on the White House steps, it would be our regrettable duty, as a bureau, in an impartial, nonpolitical and nonpartisan way to advise the Executive and Congress as to how the largest amount of garbage could be spread in the most expeditious and economical manner.[14]

Like many other influences on the civil service, that of scientific management was important and mixed. Scientific management assumed, for example, that policy goals and political directives would be clear and easy to translate into objective administrative actions. It assumed that neutral, essentially value-free (save with regard to the pursuit of efficiency) behavior on the part of career civil servants would be the norm. It assumed that government jobs really were simple and that tasks could be rigidly structured and measured. Finally, scientific management assumed that efficiency should be the primary value guiding the public service. Although all these assumptions were eventually challenged, and some discarded, the values they embodied shaped important civil service institutions and processes in significant ways and continue to do so.

Classification as Science

By the end of World War I, the federal workforce consisted of nearly one million people. The failure to differentiate between jobs in many exams and the early delegation of the examining and hiring function to agencies had resulted in a disparate set of compensation practices in the civil service and a general inability to provide equal pay for equal work. The Civil Service Commission had urged the adoption of a uniform classification system for several years; the spurt in government employment during the war heightened the commission's campaign. In 1923, the Classification Act was passed.[15] This legislation classified and graded federal positions according to duties and responsibilities. Like the Pendleton Act, the Classification Act initially applied only to a limited number of federal employees, all of whom were located in Washington. The act is important, however, for the view of public work and public organizations that it represented. The classification system, which after its creation in 1923 was not reformed until 1949, institutionalized the concept of rigid hierarchy in the American federal service. The grading of positions and their arrangement in the organization in ascending order of responsibility and authority created classic bureaucratic structures. Further, the emphasis in scientific management on clear and specific job responsibilities contributed to the creation of narrow job descriptions and strict boundaries between jobs with different responsibilities. The emphasis on standardization across organizations made the system even more inflexible.

The 1923 legislation created five compensation schedules: (1) the Professional and Scientific Service, (2) the Subprofessional Service, (3) the Clerical, Administrative, and Fiscal Service, (4) the Custodial Service, and (5) the Clerical-Mechanical Service. The act provided that "increases in compensation shall be allowed upon the attainment and maintenance of the appropriate efficiency ratings, to the next higher rate within the salary range of the grade."[16] It also provided that employees could be demoted or dismissed for poor efficiency ratings, and created a Personnel Classification Board, one of whose functions was to review and revise uniform systems of efficiency ratings.[17] The Classification Act established in law the American principle of "rank in job." This was in keeping with the perceived need for standardization and lack of flexibility; it provided that salaries or wages for each job would be determined only by the position description and the necessary qualifications for that position. This differs from the common European practice of assigning "rank in person," which emphasizes the personal qualifications of the employee filling the position and permits that person to carry rank based on those qualifications throughout the organization.

The classification system has been under nearly constant attack since its creation, but has been reformed infrequently and sporadically. As early as 1929, an analysis of the act's impact concluded that it had not created "a consistent and equitable system . . . of pay for positions involving the same work." [18] Six years later, the Commission on Inquiry of Public Service Personnel was scathing in its assessment of classification: "The most obvious fault to be found with all classifications made on the American plan is their complexity. . . . What seem to be the most trifling differences in function or difficulty are formally recognized and duly defined. . . . classifications of such complexity are to be condemned because of the fetters they place on department heads in the management of their business." [19]

In 1940, the Ramspeck Act extended the existing classification system to the entire field service. In 1949, in response to another negative analysis of classification by the first Hoover Commission, another Classification Act was passed; it reformed the system by collapsing the five occupational series into two and by moving extensive classification authority from the Civil Service Commission to the agencies. This marked another turn in the centralization/decentralization cycle that has characterized the American civil service.[20] The act also created the "supergrade" system at the top of the classified service hierarchy. Although this did not contain all the components of the British "higher civil service" model, it did recognize that the top levels of the career civil service were characterized by special policy and management expertise.

Is This Really Science? The Case of Veterans' Preference

Even with the strong influence of scientific management and standardization, the multiple personalities of the merit system continued to develop. Most of these personalities reflected influences and values quite unrelated to personnel; they caused the base system to operate in ways inconsistent with standardized principles. One of the most significant of these other personalities was veterans' preference, which had been in place since the Civil War.

The idea behind veterans' preference is simple, compelling, and essentially democratic: the nation owes a special debt to those who have fought in its wars. That debt is partially paid by providing special consideration in hiring for public jobs. Prior to the introduction of formal testing for civil service jobs, veterans were simply given priority in hiring. Following passage of the Pendleton Act, veterans were given additional points on test scores. Until 1953, veterans did not have to pass the examinations to have these bonus points added. The general scheme was that five points were added to the score of each veteran; ten points were added to the scores of those who were disabled.

Following World War I, both the growth of federal employment and the larger numbers of veterans looking for public jobs focused new attention on the practice of preferential hiring. The National Civil Service Reform League, like others, strongly opposed the expansion of the practice. In 1921 it proclaimed, for example:

> The League records its most serious apprehension at the enactment of the so-called veteran preference statutes and ordinances throughout the country. The League, while believing that the nation should suitably reward the veterans of the late war, protests any standard for admission to the public service other than ability to perform the work required as being an insidious attempt on the part of politicians to resurrect the spoils system under cover of sham patriotism.[21]

Nonetheless, spouses, widows, and mothers became eligible for preference in some circumstances; disabled veterans were permitted to move to the top of the list in others. If a veteran was not among the top three people on any list, the hiring agency had to justify the absence.

Over the long term, these practices have had a marked effect on the composition of the civil service and have further constrained discretion in federal hiring. James Fesler and Donald Kettl report that, by 1980, a third of all federal nonpostal employees were veterans.[22] Because the vast majority of veterans were white males, as was true in the armed services generally, the demographic composition of the federal bureaucracy was skewed to that component of the American population. This is a major part of the problem to which equal-opportunity and affirmative-action programs have attempted to respond.

Continuing the Challenge to Science: Special Hiring Authorities

Merit was redefined further, and made much more complex, by the creation of special hiring authorities that permitted entrance to the classified service without requiring a competitive examination to be taken. Again, the influences were politically and democratically based. Again, the impact of the add-ons was to attenuate both the neutrality and the standardization of entrance procedures to the civil service, and to challenge and change the initial foundation of merit.

Shortly after the creation of the classified civil service, the Civil Service Commission had divided it into the categories of "competitive" (for which an examination was required), "noncompetitive" (for which a noncompetitive or "unassembled" examination was required),[23] and "excepted" (for which no examination was required). The first of the special hiring authorities, Schedule A, was created to formalize these distinctions, and until 1910, all noncompetitive civil service hiring (except for political appointments) occurred under Schedule A authority. Today that authority is used primarily to hire people in certain professional occupations, such as lawyers, who are accredited or tested in some other formal way (such as by taking bar exams) and can therefore be exempted from civil service testing.

The creation of Schedule B authority in 1910 permitted noncompetitive hiring for positions that were highly specialized, or for which there was not a large labor pool to be tapped. Schedule A and B authorities have been supplemented by a plethora of more-limited special hiring authorities. Temporary and part-time appointments are common; as the complexity of tasks performed by civil servants increased, ever-larger numbers of direct-hire authorities were created to permit the targeting of specialized jobs.

Although these authorities are outside the realm of competitive merit hiring procedures, they continue the practice of centralized hiring to some extent, because the special authorities were used by agencies only with the explicit permission of the Civil Service Commission. Despite this central control, these special authorities have contributed significantly to a complex, confusing, and dysfunctional federal hiring process.

Democracy in the Public Service: Unions and Federal Employment

A critically important add-on to the civil service system, and one that has further redefined its purpose and operation, is collective bargaining. This practice differs in emphasis from both the initial content of the merit system and other add-ons: collective bargaining in government suggests that members of the civil service need to be protected from the system itself, as well as from politics.

Federal employees were permitted to join unions in 1912; the growth in federal employment during World War I and the nature of many of the jobs created in that period expanded both the size and the role of unions considerably. Again, civil service reform groups were opposed to the unions, believing they were unnecessary and could possibly contribute to hiring, promotion, and retention decisions based on grounds other than merit.[24]

Other opponents argued that, in relation to unions, government was fundamentally different from the private sector. The right to strike and the impact if a strike should occur, the scope of bargaining, and the lack of clearly identifiable management are some of the issues raised by the presence of unions in the public sector. Because management prerogatives are seriously constrained by centralized personnel functions and standardized compensation in public organizations, the relationship between unions and management is necessarily different. The implications are discussed in more detail in the next chapter.

As the United States moved toward the Great Depression and the subsequent New Deal, which would transform the federal government, the disparate influences on the civil service had created many of the qualities and problems that characterize the civil service today. The rigid hierarchical classification and compensation systems were in place; entrance to the "competitive" service was possible through a variety of avenues that did not entail competition. Patronage, the relationship of political appointees to members of the civil service, and political activities by civil servants were important issues. The emphasis placed by scientific management on neutrality, efficiency, and standardization had been profoundly challenged by the add-ons described above. An increasingly complex and expert workforce challenged the rigid application of rules and regulations so prized in the early development of the merit concept.

Merit itself had been essentially redefined by political reality, by veterans' preference, and by unions. The practice of excluding women and minorities from many "open" competitions had created a federal workforce that clearly did not reflect the population; veterans' preference had already begun to exacerbate the situation. Despite these problems, the classified service had expanded to cover a large proportion of federal employees: at the end of Herbert Hoover's term in 1932, 80 percent of the civilian positions in the executive branch were classified.[25] The level of complexity present in the merit system can be judged by the summary given in table 3.2 of key events in the system's evolution.

The Challenge Continues: Administrators and Policymakers

The next stage in the development of the civil service coincided with major historic events: the Great Depression, the New Deal, and World

Table 3.2   Key Events in the Evolution of the Merit System

1883	Pendleton Act introduces the merit concept and creates the U.S. Civil Service Commission
1887–1930s	The politics-administration dichotomy emerges
1910+	Schedule A and B special-hiring authorities complicate the hiring process
1912	Federal employees permitted to join unions
1912–1930s	Influence of scientific management in government increases, with emphasis on neutrality, economy, efficiency, and standardization
1923	Classification Act of 1923 classifies and grades federal positions according to five occupational services, establishing the principle of equal pay for equal work
1933–1945	President Franklin Roosevelt's New Deal expands government while increasing the number of excepted positions from the classified service
1936–1937	President's Committee on Administrative Management (Brownlow committee) recommends an enhanced role for presidents to manage the civil service
1939	Hatch Act prohibits federal employees from engaging in political activities
1940	Ramspeck Act extends the competitive civil service to the field service
1940s–1950s	Values of expertise, effectiveness, and responsiveness grow in importance
1944	Veterans' Preference Act codifies and extends preference in hiring for veterans
1947–1949	First Hoover Commission receives widespread attention with its emphasis on reorganizing the executive branch for greater presidential management capability and the management of personnel
1949	Classification Act of 1949 abolishes the five occupational services, simplifies schedules of grades and salaries, and creates the supergrade system
1953	President Eisenhower establishes Schedule C authority by executive order to appoint persons to positions
1953–1955	Second Hoover Commission recognizes the policy expertise of senior civil servants and argues for a special cadre of them

1958	Government Employees Training Act recognizes the importance of training and provides funding for training
1962	Federal Salary Reform Act introduces the principle of comparability with private-sector pay scales
1962	President Kennedy signs Executive Order 10988 giving federal employees the right to collective bargaining
1964	Equal Employment Opportunity Commission is created by Title VII of the Civil Rights Act of 1964 to investigate, litigate, and promulgate rules to enforce the act, which prohibits employment discrimination at the federal level on the basis of race, religion, color, sex, or national origin
1965	President Johnson signs Executive Order 11246, establishing affirmative action as the method to attain equal opportunity
1970	Federal Pay Comparability Act expands the presidential role by authorizing the president to set annual comparability pay scales without prior action by Congress
1970	Intergovernmental Personnel Act establishes a set of merit principles to improve the quality of public service at all levels and grants the Civil Service Commission a leadership role in strengthening personnel management at state and local levels
1972	Equal Employment Opportunity Act amends Title VII of the Civil Rights Act of 1964 to strengthen the authority of the Equal Employment Opportunity Commission and extend antidiscrimination provisions to state and local governments
1974	Civil Service Commission replaces the Federal Service Entrance Examination with the Professional and Administrative Career Examination
1978	Civil Service Reform Act becomes the first comprehensive reform of the merit system; abolishes the Civil Service Commission; creates the Office of Personnel Management, the Merit Systems Protection Board, and the Federal Labor Relations Authority; establishes the Senior Executive Service; institutes a pay-for-performance system for midlevel managers; curtails veterans' preference; protects whistle-blowers; reaffirms commitment to affirmative action; and creates new research-and-development authority for the Office of Personnel Management
1989	National Commission on the Public Service (Volcker Commission) releases its report on the state of the public service

Table 3.2   Continued

1990	Americans with Disabilities Act extends affirmative-action principles to those with physical and mental disabilities
1990	Office of Personnel Management devises the Administrative Careers with America examination, which includes the Individual Achievement Record
1993	Hatch Act Reform Amendments revise and simplify the 1939 Hatch Act by tightening on-the-job restrictions while easing off-duty limits on most federal and postal employees
1993	National Performance Review initiates reform efforts to improve government performance and reduce its costs
1993	President Clinton signs Executive Order 12871, creating the National Partnership Council to change collective bargaining to a system based more on collaboration and partnership

War II. As Frederick Mosher notes, the Depression made clear that "government must assume a positive role in dealing with the problems of the society and the economy," while the New Deal caused it to cease "to be merely a routine servant or a passive and reactive agent," and to become "an initiator of programs and change."[26]

This represented not only a change in size and function, but an emphasis on different values as well. The goal of efficiency did not go away, but it was joined and often superseded by the values of effectiveness and responsiveness.[27] Franklin Roosevelt clearly prized policy expertise and responsiveness above the neutral competence advocated by scientific management. In staffing many of the programs and agencies central to the New Deal, he frequently bypassed civil service testing and hiring. Paul Van Riper characterized Roosevelt's actions as "one of the most spectacular resurgences of the spoils system in American history."[28] Herbert Kaufman's assessment is more sanguine; he argues that Franklin Roosevelt was able to "kill two birds with one stone," that he "put into effect all of the programs and projects he considered vital for the welfare of the country. And he excepted the positions in these agencies from the classified service, thus enabling him to fill many of the patronage demands threatening the merit system."[29]

At the end of Franklin Roosevelt's first term, the total coverage of the classified system had declined to about 60 percent of the executive-branch workforce. Advocacy groups for good government protested loudly; Roosevelt himself was apparently concerned with coordinating and managing the now unwieldy system. In 1938, by executive order, he required that agencies establish personnel management divisions and greatly extended the competitive service. He also revised the basic civil service rules for the first time since 1903.[30]

These actions were among those recommended by the President's Committee on Administrative Management, better known as the Brownlow committee, after its chair, Louis Brownlow. The committee's report to Roosevelt was described by one scholar as "the first comprehensive reconsideration of the Presidency and the President's control of the executive branch since 1787. . . . [It] is probably the most important constitutional document of our time." [31]

The Brownlow committee firmly established the principle of good management in government. Although the link between management and the civil service system was apparently assumed to be firm, later events would demonstrate that not to be the case. For Brownlow, however, it was central. The Brownlow committee also came down firmly on the side of the president as the chief manager of government. The report stated: "Canons of efficiency require the establishment of a responsible and effective chief executive as the center of energy, direction and administrative management; the systematic organization of all activities in the hands of a qualified personnel under the direction of the chief executive; and, to aid him in this, the establishment of appropriate management and staff agencies." [32]

The significance of the management role that Brownlow assigned to the president, and the implications for the role of Congress, are important milestones in the continuing drama of "joint custody." The report recommended that the president's immediate staff be expanded, that the Bureau of the Budget be made more directly accountable to the president, that the agencies in the executive branch be reorganized into twelve major departments, and that the president be given improved planning and fiscal management capabilities.

Although Congress acted on few of Brownlow's recommendations immediately—Roosevelt and the Congress were not on good terms at that point—the nature of the debate about who was responsible for the civil service and to whom it was responsible was reshaped. Peri Arnold provides an apt summary: "The Brownlow Committee assumed that the interests of good administration and the President's interests were overlapping, if not identical." [33] That assumption has guided the management and direction efforts of every president since Franklin Roosevelt; it continues to be a topic of fierce debate. Its premise that good government is defined by responsiveness to the president and that the role of the civil service in governance is confined to that responsiveness not only turns earlier analyses of the relationship of politics to merit around, but substantially alters definitions of neutrality and effectiveness.

The Brownlow definition of the presidential role, then, contained two elements of critical importance to the civil service. First, the constitutional issue related to the balance between Congress and the president with regard to the direction of the civil service was not addressed; the role of Congress was not discussed in any detail whatsoever. Clearly, this set the stage for future debate and for congressional response.

Second, the peculiar relationship between politics and administration resurfaced in a slightly different guise. The issue of responsiveness was not couched in terms of neutral competence, or even in terms of responsiveness to political direction, but in terms of giving the president adequate authority and resources to be a good *manager*. Despite the controversies earlier in Roosevelt's term about a return to spoils, about packing the Supreme Court, and about other actions that looked suspiciously like political excess, his managerial role was viewed as separable from his political role.

That is not to say that no one was concerned about the continued potential for undue political influence on the civil service. In 1939, Congress passed the Hatch Act, which prohibited federal employees from participating in partisan political activities. In 1940, the second Hatch Act extended the provisions to employees of state and local governments that received federal funds. As Benda and Rosenbloom note, "The Hatch Act originally was based on a reasonably coherent concept of what a public service should *not* be."[34] The view was in line with that of the earlier reformers: partisan politics, given the opportunity, would corrupt the civil service, using its members for partisan electoral and patronage purposes.

In addition to the new emphasis on political direction, there was also a new focus on expanding the civil service based on its traditional role and rules. The passage of the Ramspeck Act in 1940 provided for the extension of the competitive civil service to more than 182,000 permanent positions. As the Civil Service Commission noted, "it authorized the President to sweep away virtually all of the exceptions which had accumulated since 1883."[35] Using the authority provided him by the act, President Roosevelt further extended the merit program and eliminated some of the duplicative and conflicting rules and regulations that had grown around it in the preceding years. At the time of World War II, then, the federal civil service again appeared to be on a solid merit footing, but it clearly reflected the major influences of the previous fifty years: narrow standardization, rigidity, and a strong emphasis on technical competence. Wallace Sayre termed this "the triumph of techniques over purpose," and added, "In the public field, especially, quantitative devices have overshadowed qualitative. Standardization and uniformity have been enshrined as major virtues. Universal (and therefore arbitrary) methods have been preferred to experiment and variety. From the perspective of the clientele . . . these traits increasingly connote rigidity, bureaucracy; institutionalism—and they are now beginning to invoke a reciprocal system of formal and informal techniques of evasion." [36]

Post–World War II: Examining the Elephant

World War II severely tested the ability of the federal government to deliver services effectively and efficiently. Government employment grew from about eight hundred thousand in 1938 to nearly four million by 1945. As in World War I, many of the appointments were made under temporary authority and bypassed civil service testing and lists. Although the War Department (now the Department of Defense) advised Congress that it needed to bypass the Civil Service Commission entirely in its civilian hiring, the commission retained its central personnel authority. It did, however, decentralize the recruiting and examining function substantially.

In 1944, the passage of the Veterans' Preference Act codified and extended preference in hiring for veterans and some members of their families, created an appeals process whereby veterans could go to directly to the Civil Service Commission to appeal removal and other adverse actions, and required that veterans with performance ratings of "good" or above be given preference when any reductions in force became necessary. This had a major impact on the postwar civil service. In 1949, 47 percent of federal employees in the continental United States had some kind of veterans' preference; this was up from only 16 percent at the end of the war.[37]

Following the death of Franklin Roosevelt and the move into the presidency by Harry S. Truman, the federal service faced both reductions in force and problems with management. President Truman requested and received new reorganization authority from Congress, but the massive debt, overlapping responsibilities of agencies, and general need to adapt to a postwar economy mandated a more thorough examination of the organization and operation of the federal government.

In 1947, with President Truman's support, Congress created the first Hoover Commission. The choice of former president Herbert Hoover to head the commission demonstrated the level of attention that Congress intended to give its activities. At the same time, the choice of the conservative Hoover suggested that the commission would assume a critical and controversial stance. It did.

The First Hoover Commission: The Elephant Does Not Work

The foreword to the Hoover Commission's report clearly states the nature of the inquiry; its language is somewhat reminiscent of the passion expressed by the earlier reformers: "The average citizen has become uncomfortably conscious of the vast size of our government. We all want and expect many services from the government, to be sure, but we are baffled by its magnitude and frightened by its cost. Instinctively, we see a possible danger to democracy itself." [38]

Hoover divided his commission into twenty-four task forces; they issued nineteen reports to Congress. In an unusual move, Hoover also created the Citizens' Committee for the Hoover Reports. The committee's motto was "Better Government for a Better Price." It was a national organization, with many local groups and a well-organized and effective public relations capability.

In relation to the civil service, the committee's assessment of existing procedures was harsh. Classification was a particular target; the commission recommended that it be less narrow and rigid and much more simple. The *management* of personnel was again emphasized, and reorganization of the executive branch to give the president better management capability and the Congress better oversight ability was suggested. The management authority of departmental secretaries was also examined; the commission recommended that it be expanded.

The initial Hoover Commission Report was not the first report to recognize that management of employees was as important as their protection from political abuse, nor was it the first to observe that the federal personnel system's emphasis on centralization and standardization did not contribute to good management. It was the first, however, to receive widespread attention and support for its recommendations, both in Congress and among the citizens.

By the time Dwight Eisenhower was elected president in 1952, the foundation of the civil service was intact, but it was the target of frequent criticism. The system itself had resisted most efforts to dilute its rigid structure and hierarchy, and merit had become inextricably bound to both. The cycle of centralization and decentralization had been well established in the federal civil service. The relationship between politics and administration had become unclear. The complicated programs of the New Deal and the demands of the war had seriously challenged the tenets of both scientific management and the politics-administration dichotomy, but no suitable alternative had been found. The early view that merit was possible only if politics was excluded had been transformed into a more sophisticated argument that both merit and effectiveness were enhanced if politics played a central role. The Hatch Act had ensured that blatant political abuse was much less likely to occur. Nonetheless, how the role for politics—and particularly for presidential politics and direction of the civil service—was to be defined was becoming a key issue for the civil service.

Further, a different view of the role of the classified civil service and its top career managers in politics and policy had started to emerge. Norton Long summarized that view in the phrase "the lifeblood of administration is power!"[39] in 1949. Proponents argued that the nature of modern politics and policy precluded the exclusion of bureaucrats from key decisions and discussions; their expertise was central to the proper analysis and understanding of policy options. This was a vision of "shared power"; the public service was to be viewed as a partner in policy. This view discarded old questions about how administrators could be ideal neutral civil servants, and raised new ones about the proper and possible limits on growing bureaucratic power. Frederick Mosher observed:

> The accretion of specialization and of technological and social complexity seems to be an irreversible trend, one that leads to increasing dependence upon the protected, appointive public service, thrice removed from direct democracy. Herein lies the central and underlying problem . . . how can a public service so constituted be made to operate in a manner compatible with democracy? How can we be assured that a highly differentiated body of public employees will act in the interests of all the people, will be an instrument of all the people?[40]

The Elephant from Another Angle: Politics and Administration Revisited

The central issue of bureaucratic control and discretion was addressed in two important ways during the Eisenhower presidency. The second Hoover Commission formally recognized the policy expertise of senior civil servants and the need to incorporate that expertise into decision making in some more systematic way. It recognized the tension between political appointees and these top careerists as well, noting the vast differences in experience and perspective each brought to the relationship. It laid the groundwork for important future reform when it argued strongly for the creation of a special cadre of senior civil servants who could cross over into policy debate and decisions, but also maintain civil service status. The British higher service and the enormous discretion it enjoyed was the obvious model. Most of these recommendations were not acted on during the Eisenhower presidency, but they became an integral part of future debates.

Eisenhower himself was responsible for the other major development of his presidency. He came to the White House comfortable with the military chain-of-command model. He expected to have his orders carried out and was chagrined and frustrated to discover that getting results from the large federal bureaucracy was not so straightforward a process. Part of the problem, he believed, was that the ability of the president to place political appointees inside executive agencies had been too severely constrained. In greatly oversimplified form, the political management model in place when Eisenhower assumed the presidency was the one pictured in figure 3.2.

The truncated pyramid in figure 3.2 models the relationship of political appointees to career civil servants in most large federal agencies. The top of the pyramid is filled with political appointees, primarily those appointed by the president and subject to Senate confirmation, but also some "supergrade" (GS16–18) appointees. In the Eisenhower administration, that total number was about 433.[41] The bottom of the pyramid is composed of career civil servants, with the top part of that section filled by senior career managers and experts at the supergrade level. Eisenhower was frustrated by the gap between the two; he did not feel that there were enough political appointees to ensure responsiveness to presidential direction. Consequently, he created Schedule C by executive order. Schedule C gave the president authority to appoint persons he trusted and who shared his policy views to policy-sensitive positions inside the agencies. Appointees could be placed wherever policy-sensitive discussions could occur or needed special attention. Schedule C appointees, therefore, could be personal secretaries for top-level appointees, chauffeurs for those same people, or midlevel (to GS15) managers. Eisenhower used this authority sparingly. However, as presidential management strategies became more focused on controlling, rather than directing, the bureaucracy, Schedule Cs became an important part of the strategy and a much larger proportion of appointees.

Presidential efforts to manage the civil service have been a significant part of civil service history and reform for the past thirty years. The complexity of that endeavor, the dramatically changing nature of the civil

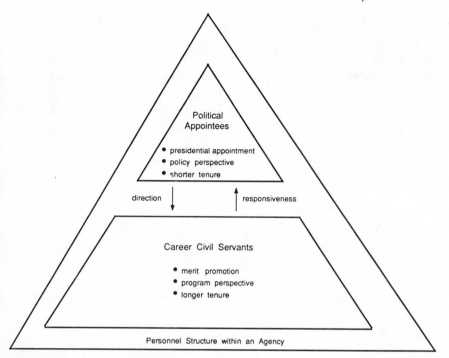

Figure 3.2   Relationship of Political Appointees to Civil Service Personnel

service being directed and managed, and new views of management are the topics of the next chapters. As those chapters will demonstrate, the add-ons and the changing views of the role of the public service described above had become an important part of the problem. The add-ons had contributed to the complexity of the system and to a serious lack of coherence in its structures and processes. Standardization was combined with special attention; neutrality was combined with special characteristics; rules were increasingly becoming a mechanism for controlling the bureaucracy, rather than a means for ordering its activities.

The serious tension between discretion, particularly for senior civil servants, and presidential direction and control was increasingly clear. The shifting balance between presidential and congressional direction created additional strains and discomfort. Even though it was clear that the substantial expertise and skill that the members of the civil service represented was a significant policy resource, exercise of the power that resource created was generally viewed with alarm. The nature of the role the merit system and the civil service could play in governance was less clear. The paradox of merit in the American system of government had become central to many policy debates: the civil service and its members were fundamental to the ability to address important problems. But neither the civil servants nor the system that recruited, motivated, and rewarded them were looked upon with favor and confidence by elected officials and many citizens. This was due in part to an inability to understand the system; even those within its confines were sometimes puzzled by the many provisions and procedures it included. The next chapter discusses the highlights of some of the complexities and their implications.

Chapter Four

Adding

On to

the System

The description of the federal merit system in the preceding chapters demonstrates the intricate relationship between politics and merit, as well as the extent to which the size and capacity of the system have been responsive to major historical and economic events. It is equally important to understand the extent to which the incremental development of the system, and the frequently competing influences on that development, worked to create a set of programs and policies that do not have the coherence or mutual purpose that the term "system" most often implies. The merit system is fragmented in many ways; the fragmentation is attributable in part to the incremental and political nature of its development.

Another reason for the system's fragmentation and lack of coherence is the overlay of a civil service system on a system for democratic governance. Despite the long-term emphasis on the core of centralization and standardization, many exceptions to both have been created in the history of the merit system.

Some of these exceptions are major. The foreign service and the postal service, for example, have entire personnel systems separate from those of the general classified service. Other exceptions are more narrow, but still significant. In spite of the emphasis on standardized classification and compensation, by the end of the 1980s there were at least thirty different pay systems associated with the civil service. Still other exceptions appear modest: as Peace Corps volunteers began returning to the United States in the late 1960s, for example, a special direct-hiring authority was created to facilitate their entrance into the classified civil service. By itself, this does not seem important. By 1985, however, there were so many direct-hire authorities that they were difficult to count. In 1987, more than a third of the new members of the civil service entered through excepted authorities rather than standardized examinations.[1]

The dance between standardization and exception has been a hallmark of the civil service in the past forty years. It has been so consistent that exceptions to the rule are now as significant as the basic rules themselves. That is the conundrum of the modern civil service. The exceptions have been just that: exceptions. They have been added to an existing framework rather than altering it. The fundamental merit principles of entrance through neutral competitive examination, promotion and reward based on performance, and protection from partisan political abuse have generally remained intact, but have been reinterpreted, expanded, and, in some cases, contradicted in the process.

Further, the exceptions that have been added in the past forty years have been responses to different values and objectives from those that influenced earlier additions to the merit system. In the cases of veterans' preference and special hiring authorities, some components of rigid standardization were discarded early. More recently, democratic values such as social equity and diversity have become closely entwined with civil service activities and procedures. Unions, collective bargaining, and the rights of public employees to organize are now significant concerns. The courts have become active and influential in the oversight and interpretation of civil service and public management activities.[2] Equal employment opportunity and affirmative action have been added in an effort to make the federal bureaucracy more broadly representative of the citizens it serves.

The concept of merit has changed; the add-ons to merit listed in table 4.1 have caused it to become less clear and, many argue, less relevant to the activities involved in managing government. For better or worse, earlier reforms responded in some way to the objectives of efficiency and economy and were linked to a specific view of administrative activities and outcomes. The new additions to the system responded to the objectives of individual rights, equity, and effectiveness and were not tied to either administrative or managerial processes, except as they existed to serve larger democratic purposes. The conflicts between the new add-ons, as well as between the add-ons and the older system, created an organization with serious internal tensions and few obvious measures of good or effective performance.

In addition, concerns about managing public programs were begin-

Table 4.1   Changes Complicating the Merit System

Affirmative-action programs

Classification systems

Collective bargaining

Compensation rules and regulations

Court decisions

Equal-employment-opportunity programs

Excepted personnel systems

Labor/management relations

Management by objectives

Pay for performance

Performance appraisals

Public service orientation

Recruitment practices

Separate pay systems

Special hiring authorities

Testing and examining functions

Total quality management

Training and development

Veterans' preference

---

ning to be overlaid on the civil service. The technical view so pervasive in the theory of scientific management was altered first by the emerging concern with presidential direction, and later by the growing awareness of the complex policy role of the career civil service. More recently, efforts to increase flexibility and responsiveness have again emphasized the transfer of private-sector methods and practices: management by objective, pay for performance, and total quality management have become prevalent in public systems. All assume a level of managerial authority and discretion quite at odds with the constraints and controls of civil service systems, with their emphases on applying rules and regulations, rather than proactive problem solving.

Most of this happened, however, by default, rather than as a result of conscious decisions or serious examination. As was the case with the incremental development of the core system, the new directions have come when politics allowed, in response to external social, economic, and political influences. The pursuit of efficiency has gradually been joined, and occasionally replaced, by the need to be effective, not only in the sense of program delivery and service, but in the sense of serving democracy. This transformation from "civil service" to "public service" illustrates the normative aspects of the contemporary civil service. In Hugh Heclo's terms, it is not about administration, but "a statement of what should be."[3]

A brief description of the major additions to the base already described will help clarify the complexity and tensions of the contemporary merit system. The following summaries are necessarily simplified; in the early 1990s there were more than six thousand pages of rules and regulations related to the civil service. Only the most dedicated personnel officers understood all of them. It is my purpose here to explore the broad parameters and intent, but also to clarify the extent to which the system's incremental growth from a standardized and bureaucratic base made it increasingly difficult to manage and direct. Of equal significance, the inconsistent, and sometimes incoherent, development of the system obscured the original objectives and left an increasingly unclear view of what the civil service could or should be. Finally, but not least, virtually nothing in the system supports and rewards good *management,* rather than administration. The National Performance Review's report summarized the problem in these terms: "Human resource administration is forms driven, labor intensive, and time consuming. Managers and personnelists alike labor under rules and procedures requiring the meticulous handling of paper. With incomprehensible procedural and regulatory requirements, managers shy away from learning or accepting responsibility for human resource management."[4]

Classification and Compensation

The Classification Act of 1923 and the revisions contained in the Classification Act of 1949 have already been discussed. The primary effect of these acts was narrowly to describe civil service jobs and occupations in a standardized way, to order them hierarchically within and across organizations, and to link each level of the organization and the jobs it contained to grades, which were in turn linked to standard wages and salaries.

At the time of the passage of each act, the principle of "equal pay for equal work" was emphasized. As the system grew and became more differentiated, blue-collar wages were linked to local market rates. Other jobs, however, were standardized not only across organizations, but across all regions of the United States. A revenue agent for the Internal

Revenue Service received the same salary in Birmingham, Alabama, or Pierre, South Dakota, for example, as she did in New York City.

As early as 1935, the Commission on Inquiry of Public Service Personnel reported that the principles of "equal pay for equal work" and "performance based on efficiency" were difficult to put into operation and were unlikely to be implemented in a satisfactory way if they continued to be linked to a flawed classification system. The basic system remained in place, however, with any pay-related legislation providing only for pay raises. The Federal Employees' Pay Acts of 1945 and 1946 together increased pay for many jobs by 30 percent.[5] The Classification Act of 1949 also provided for a pay increase. It is important to note that, in these cases, Congress needed to pass legislation specifically for the purpose of increasing civil service salaries. There was no other mechanism for change.

In 1962, the Federal Salary Reform Act significantly altered the pay-setting process for white-collar employees. The act gave the president a major role in the salary issue for the first time. On the advice of the Civil Service Commission and the Bureau of the Budget, the president became able to recommend salary scales for the civil service. The principle of comparability with private-sector pay scales was now included in the pay formula. A caveat is necessary: "comparable to" has never meant "equal to" in the federal service. A long-term, but generally unspoken, rule has been that public employees will be paid at rates below those of their private-sector counterparts. This is variously explained in terms of more-generous and more-stable benefits in the public sector, more-limited public funds, and the altruistic benefits that accrue to those in the public service: doing good for others is its own reward.[6]

In 1970, the Federal Pay Comparability Act expanded the presidential role by delegating to the president "the authority to set annual comparability pay scales without prior action on the part of Congress."[7] The Civil Service Commission and the Bureau of the Budget (now the Office of Management and Budget) act as the president's agents for this activity. The system is complicated. Federal-employee unions are involved in the early stages of the annual determination, and the process is reviewed each year by an external independent group, the Advisory Committee on Federal Pay, which not only reviews the activities of the Civil Service Commission and the OMB, but makes its own recommendations to the president.

Significantly, the pay of Congress enters directly into the equation because it is statutorily linked to the pay of the top members of the civil service and the appointed executives. That involves a different process for pay recommendation and pay setting, in which Congress votes on its own salary increases at the same time it votes on increases for top-level executives and members of the judiciary. Since 1967, the Commission on Executive, Legislative, and Judicial Salaries, commonly called the Quadrennial Commission because it meets every four years, has recommended appropriate salary increases to the president. Based on this recommendation, the president then sends to Congress a proposal for new pay rates. These rates become effective unless Congress specifically disapproves them. The president is not required to send a new rate forward, however, nor will the president necessarily propose the amount recommended by the Quadrennial Commission. The difficulties this can create, both in terms of capping the salaries of the executives if the members of Congress do not wish to take the political risk of increasing their own salaries, and in terms of creating salary compression within the ranks of the civil service, are discussed in more detail in the chapter on civil service reform.

Both the process for determining federal pay and the amount of pay have come under frequent attack. This is particularly true for senior career managers and executives. When the National Commission on the Public Service (the Volcker Commission) released its report on the state of the public service in 1989, it noted, "Pay setting for top level federal executives follows an historic pattern of lengthy periods of stagnation and relative decline of the purchasing power of salaries. Even with three mechanisms for increasing Congressional pay—by statute, Quadrennial Commission processes, and annual increase—the purchasing power of pay for federal elected and appointed executives decreased by 35 percent from 1969 to 1988." [8]

Testing and Recruitment

The procedures for recruiting and testing personnel for the federal civil service also changed in the postwar period. The examining function had gone through several cycles of being delegated to regional boards or to the agencies, only to be recentralized when the Civil Service Commission became dissatisfied with the standards and procedures being employed in a decentralized setting. The holding of examinations was never a guarantee that positions were available; rather, it was a screening process intended to create a reservoir of appropriate talent for civil service positions as they became available. The Commission on Inquiry of Public Service Personnel called this a "bad practice" in 1935; [9] the concern was that since the examination was basically a pass/fail test, the pool would contain large numbers of minimally qualified persons who, lacking better employment opportunities, would "wait out" the chance for a federal job. The commission also bitterly attacked the practice of veterans' preference, calling it "indefensible when judged by the criterion of fair play." [10]

In both world wars, the testing function was bypassed and thousands of people were appointed through temporary procedures. This same situation occurred during the Korean War. In 1954, President Eisenhower established the "career-conditional" system through executive order. That new system recognized, in the words of the Civil Service Commission, that "not all persons who enter Government service intend to spend the rest of their working lives in that service, and [that] Government may not have continuing jobs for all those who may be needed during an emergency." [11] The executive order created a three-year period of conditional status, after which, if the employee's performance had been satisfactory, full career status and career benefits were attained.

This program permitted the Civil Service Commission to downsize after large buildups, but also to begin a regular recruiting effort aimed at particular groups. The first group targeted was college graduates. In 1954, the Civil Service Commission created a consolidated entrance examination aimed at this group. The new examination replaced more than one hundred earlier examinations and included essentially all professional positions (except for engineering and some sciences) in the civil service. It was called the Federal Service Entrance Examination (FSEE), and it remained in use until 1974.

In 1974, the FSEE was replaced by the Professional and Administrative Career Examination (PACE). PACE was intended to be a more sophisticated exam with a better ability to identify those who would be successful civil servants. As with the FSEE, its primary purpose was to serve a sifting function that would screen out substantial numbers of applicants while building a strong candidate pool. The PACE was extremely successful in that regard, but the outcome was troublesome. In 1976, there were 222,000 applicants for the examination; 51 percent of those passed. Seven percent of those who passed were appointed to jobs, so test scores in the high nineties were required if the applicant was to be likely to obtain a job. [12]

Statistics detailing the characteristics of those who took the examination compared to those who passed it revealed that white candidates were passing and obtaining jobs in disproportionate numbers. In *Leuvano v. Campbell* (later *Leuvano v. Devine*), representatives of minority groups sued, arguing that PACE was a discriminatory examination and that the "neutral" entrance examination was clearly not neutral in its impact. Although the PACE accounted for only 35 percent of hires to administrative and professional positions when the suit was filed, its familiarity and symbolic significance made it an important recruiting mechanism.[13] Further, PACE appointees frequently moved into managerial positions later in their careers; the discriminatory entrance impact was therefore reflected in the upper levels of public organizations as well.

Although the Carter administration agreed to a consent decree that would have phased the examination out gradually, the Reagan administration simply abolished the exam. For several years in the 1980s, agencies and potential applicants were left to deal with other appointment authorities and entrance procedures. The most heavily used authority was the obscure Schedule B.

For some agencies, particularly those that continued to hire fairly large numbers of new employees during this period (such as the Internal Revenue Service and the Department of Defense), the decentralized and flexible processes afforded by Schedule B worked fairly well. Those agencies developed their own recruiting and testing procedures and were apparently successful in targeting women and minority candidates. Limited empirical evidence suggests that they increased hiring in these areas from previous PACE levels.[14]

For other agencies and for many job applicants, however, the experience with Schedule B was not so positive. Agencies with limited opportunity to hire did not develop their own recruiting and testing abilities. They were forced to deal with jobs on a case-by-case basis and had difficulty locating prospective applicants. The applicants, for their part, did not know where to apply for federal jobs in the absence of the centralized testing mechanism.

The Merit Systems Protection Board reviewed the hiring that had occurred under Schedule B and determined that it did not meet the "free and open competition" standard of the merit system. The director of the Office of Personnel Management, Constance Horner, agreed, calling the hiring system "legally trammeled and intellectually confused" and noting that it did not fulfill "the spirit of our mandate to hire the most meritorious candidates." [15]

At the end of the 1980s, the Office of Personnel Management (the successor agency to the Civil Service Commission) was ordered to stop using Schedule B authority and to devise a new centralized examination. That examination, the Administrative Careers with America (ACWA) examination, was introduced in 1990. The new examination series includes tests for the six occupational groups that hire the most extensively. It is also notable for including the Individual Achievement Record (IAR), which details individual achievements and activities and which is considered along with the standardized test score.

The issue of centralized testing and examining versus a more decentralized model is a crucial one for the federal government. Many organizations, confronted with rapidly changing technology and a nearly constant need for new employee skills and knowledge, argue that a centralized system is too slow and cumbersome to meet their needs effectively. Other organizations argue that they do not have the capacity to carry out the recruiting and testing function themselves. A 1990 analysis by the Office of Personnel Management bears this out: the OPM found that the federal government's ability to recruit on college campuses was severely constrained by limited funding, by limited advertising, and by almost no training for the recruiting function. Half the organizations the OPM studied reported that they had no college recruiting brochures or advertising budgets; 80 percent of the college recruiters said they had been given no training to do their jobs.[16]

The effectiveness of the new ACWA examination is not yet clear and the federal government has not hired extensively in the years since it has been implemented. The extent to which a relatively rigid and centralized testing system continues to meet the needs of a dramatically changing federal workforce is one of the issues addressed by the recommendations of the National Performance Review. If decentralization is deemed more effective, serious attention must be paid to the ability of the individual agencies to carry out the recruiting and testing tasks that will be delegated to them, as well as to the extent to which those activities can be, or need to be, monitored for conformance with general standards and merit guidelines.

Equal Employment Opportunity and Affirmative Action

Compensation, recruiting, and testing practices were supposed to adhere to standards of fairness and equity, but they also responded to other democratic values and to market and demographic pressures. These influences are not necessarily compatible. One of the most important add-ons to recruiting and hiring came in response to an emergent concern for *social* equity and for a public service that was representative of the population in general. This issue was certainly not new; Thomas Jefferson expressed concern about the lack of representativeness in the federal service during his presidency.

Two broad influences converged in the 1960s, however, and created new demands for change. First, the civil-rights movement emphasized the glaring inequities that existed in American society. The Civil Rights Act of 1964 prohibited discrimination based on race, color, religion, gender, or national origin. This was extended by Executive Order 11246, signed by President Johnson in 1965, to all employers and subcontractors with federal contracts.[17] The Equal Pay Act of 1963 specifically prohibited pay discrimination based on gender.

The second major influence was that of veterans' preference. The veterans from World War II and the Korean War had frequently turned to the federal government for employment; the benefits provided by veterans' preference made this a logical and relatively easy option. At that time the U.S. military was primarily composed of white males, however; the net effect was to create a federal bureaucracy that reflected the military and not American society in general. The formal effects of veterans' preference were exacerbated by less formal, but no less concrete, patterns of discrimination based on gender and race in hiring in many federal agencies.[18] The resulting lack of representativeness was in direct conflict with the objectives of both civil-rights legislation and President Johnson's executive order.

Two solutions were proposed. Equal employment opportunity (EEO) was intended to ensure that all citizens were given fair and equal opportunities in testing, hiring, promotion, and retention procedures. Affirmative action (AA), created by President Johnson's executive order, required employers to take positive action to redress past inequities by making special efforts to recruit and hire underrepresented groups. AA was given a statutory basis by the Equal Opportunity Employment Act of 1972.

Affirmative action is a controversial policy that has often been challenged on the grounds that it creates quota systems for employers. Other analyses of affirmative action center on its movement away from the "neutral" standards of the merit system. Mosher does not directly address AA, but offers the following analysis of representative bureaucracy: "If individual officers are to be chosen to represent certain interests and points of view, clearly a merit system premised on efficiency and mastery of knowledge and skills appropriate to specific jobs is not adequate."[19]

Mosher's perspective is, not surprisingly, somewhat contradictory to that of the Civil Service Commission, which, in discussing equal employment opportunity, offers the following assessment of its compatibility with the merit system:

The impression is left among some that equal opportunity is the antithesis of merit. As a matter of fact, it had been the entire purpose of the merit system all along to focus on the qualifications and performance of individuals and to guard against either favoritism or discrimination founded on race, religion, political affiliation, sex, or other factors extraneous to getting the Government's work done more effectively. . . . [The intention of EEO was] not to negate merit but to make more certain that it was truly being achieved.[20]

Affirmative-action principles have been extended to cover age as well as physical and mental disabilities, the latter in the Americans with Disabilities Act of 1990.

Although the Equal Employment Opportunity Commission was created in 1964, its responsibilities did not formally include enforcement of EEO and AA provisions in the federal government. That responsibility resided with the Civil Service Commission until the Civil Service Reform Act of 1978 (discussed in chapter 5) transferred it to the Equal Employment Opportunity Commission.

The issues of equal employment opportunity and affirmative action have been vigorously pursued in the courts. *Griggs v. Duke Power Company* was the first major Supreme Court ruling and is a landmark decision. In that 1971 case, the Court ruled that congressional intent in the Civil Rights Act of 1964 was clearly to "achieve equality of employment opportunity and to remove barriers that have operated in the past to favor an identifiable group of white employees over other employees."[21]

The Court placed responsibility with the employer to demonstrate that any entrance or testing requirements were clearly job related, and were not intended to discriminate. This interpretation of the law generally held for the next fifteen years. Frank Thompson summarizes the time succinctly: "The 1970s and 1980s saw the Supreme Court issue several other rulings directly related to affirmative action for racial minorities. Until 1989, these rulings generally reflected continuity in policy. None of the court decisions represented the bold step toward social equity represented in *Griggs*. But neither did they feature a significant gutting of this commitment."[22]

In 1989 a major shift occurred. Again, Frank Thompson summarizes: "No one decision dealt a death blow to affirmative action. Certainly, none overturned *Griggs*. But taken as a whole, the rulings sent a signal that the Supreme Court would be looking for reasons not to side with minority plaintiffs in equal employment cases."[23] One of the most important of these cases was *Wards Cove Packing Company v. Frank Atonio*, in which the Court placed the burden of proof firmly on those claiming discrimination, rather than on the employer. The Court also found that discrimination could *not* be demonstrated by statistics showing larger numbers of minorities in low-level, unskilled jobs than in higher-level jobs in the organization.[24]

Indirectly, this case points to another issue related to equal employment opportunity: most remedies have been directed at entrance to an organization. The ability of women and minorities to move up through an organization to more-complex jobs, as well as to positions of authority, has been less frequently addressed. Some recent analyses, however, have demonstrated the critical impact of theoretically neutral internal processes on underrepresented minorities.

The comparable-worth controversies in both public and private organizations have shown, for example, that jobs held primarily by women have traditionally carried lower salaries than those held mainly by men.[25] This has been due, at least in part, to job descriptions and classification standards that systematically placed "women's jobs" at lower levels. In addition, educational requirements and other threshold criteria for promotion or for movement up a career ladder have limited opportunities for minorities and women.[26] Internal labor-market mechanisms have helped create organizations in which these groups are disproportionately represented at the bottom of the organization and are represented in small numbers, or not at all, at the top.

In public organizations, these practices are given the force of law by civil service rules and procedures. The impact is exacerbated by other civil service rules, such as the "last in, first out" seniority rule. Unless early-retirement programs are in effect, the last persons hired are the first people to be fired when budget and staff cuts occur. Again, women and minorities are disproportionately affected.

The federal civil service and federal organizations provide good evidence of the impact. Although African Americans and other minority groups made up 17.6 percent of the national workforce and 21.8 percent of the federal workforce in 1989, they were present in limited numbers at the middle and top levels of federal organizations.[27] J. Edward Kellough and David Rosenbloom report, for example, that in grades GS9 through GS12, the entry-level management policy and management positions, African Americans held 8.1 percent of the jobs in 1978 and 10.6 percent in 1986. Hispanics held 2.5 percent in 1978 and 4.1 percent in 1986. Women held 24.4 percent in 1978 and 34.5 percent in 1986.[28] In 1993, federal civilian employee statistics showed that the workforce was 44 percent women and 28.1 percent minority groups, with 16.8 percent African Americans and 5.6 percent Hispanics.[29] In the Senior Executive

Service, the executive cadre of the civil service, 12 percent of the members were women in 1991; 8 percent were minorities.[30]

At this stage of its development, then, the civil service system is as important for how it treats people once they are in it as it is for how it controls and limits entry. Just as the earlier standardized examinations created obstacles for many citizens outside the system, classification, career development, and promotion policies have created subtle, but significant, obstacles for the limited number of underrepresented minorities who made it over the first hurdle.

Labor/Management Relations and Collective Bargaining

The right of public employees to organize and to join unions has been recognized since 1912.[31] Government employees were not, however, covered by early legislation, such as the Wagner Act of 1935, which extended collective-bargaining rights to union members, or the Taft-Hartley Act of 1947, which prohibited unions from engaging in unfair labor practices. There has always been a sense that public-sector unions are different and that the reality of public employment in some ways abrogates both the need and the right to rely on collective bargaining as a solution.

Some analysts have argued, however, that because public employees are denied the right to engage in partisan politics on their own behalf and lack other means of protecting their interests, public-sector unions serve an important purpose. A large number of public-sector employees are now members of unions, although the percentage of unionized employees varies dramatically from organization to organization and between levels of government. The U.S. Postal Service is an example of a highly unionized organization; organizations such as the Department of Housing and Urban Development have few union members. Local government employees such as firefighters and police are also extensively organized. Fesler and Kettl note that a third of all union members are government employees; 60 percent of federal workers are represented by unions through collective bargaining.[32]

This activity was sanctioned formally in 1962, during the Kennedy administration. Executive Order 10988 gave federal employees the right to bargain collectively; many state governments quickly followed. Additional executive orders expanded employee rights and the role of unions; statutory authority for these provisions did not occur until 1978, when the Civil Service Reform Act (CSRA) was passed. Federal employees in the classified service may still not bargain over wages and benefits, which are determined by Congress and governed by classification and compensation rules and regulations.

Federal employees are also not permitted to strike. A famous test of this rule was provided early in the Reagan administration, when President Reagan fired air-traffic controllers after their union, the Professional Air Traffic Controllers' Organization (PATCO), called a strike. That event clearly demonstrated the problems inherent in collective bargaining in a public setting.

Air-traffic controllers are employed by the Federal Aviation Administration, an agency in the Department of Transportation. They serve a critical public-safety function at every major airport in the United States. Safe and reasonable working conditions are fundamental to their effective job performance. Adequate, and perhaps superior, pay is essential to attracting and retaining well-trained and committed controllers. What is the best way to achieve all these conditions? For the nearly eleven thousand members of PATCO, the answer was collective bargaining and, in 1981, a strike. President Reagan's swift response suggested a different answer and a different view of the rights of public employees.

Fesler and Kettl observe that the "issues posed by unionization of public employees run deep," and that among those issues are the right to strike, the question of "who are the bargainers," and the serious tensions between collective bargaining and the civil service system itself.[33] President Reagan's action in the PATCO strike demonstrated that the "management team" in a public organization is defined differently from one in the private sector. Obviously, it involves agency management, but it also contains personnel representatives from the agency and from the central personnel agency. It can also involve the president and Congress. Agreements reached by the first group can be, and often are, overruled by the latter two players. For all the reasons outlined above, and because labor/management relations in the federal government have most often been adversarial, collective bargaining has remained somewhat tangential to reform efforts, in spite of its extensive coverage. It was, in fact, not given a statutory base until passage of the CSRA in 1978; it was supported by executive order until that time. In combination with the limited number of issues and decisions that can be bargained for in a civil service system, these realities have allowed only limited development of a cooperative model of collective bargaining at the federal level.

The National Partnership Council, created by executive order by President Clinton as part of his "reinventing government" initiative, proposed to change the essentially confrontational collective-bargaining model to one that is based on collaboration and partnership. The Clinton administration argued that new government priorities and objectives mandated improved communication and coordination; the success of the council's effort remains unclear.

Training and Development

Other add-ons to the core system have had a less significant impact than those described above, but are important nonetheless. One example is training and development. For much of the history of the civil service, there were more qualified applicants for federal jobs than there were jobs available. Paul Van Riper observes that before World War II, "the excess of applicants compared to available jobs had suggested to both Congress and many administrators that extensive in-service training programs were essentially wasteful." [34] Although training was necessary during the war and extensive retraining occurred after it had ended, there was little effort to address the training and development needs of the civil service generally. The first Hoover Commission was strongly critical of this absence.

It was not until the presidency of Dwight Eisenhower, with the serious commitment to training and development he brought from his military career, that formal action was taken. In Eisenhower's first term, the Federal Training Policy Statement directed the Civil Service Commission to develop training plans and opportunities for the entire federal workforce. In Eisenhower's second term, the Government Employees' Training Act of 1958 was passed. The act provided funds for agency and centralized training programs, but was only moderately successful in energizing training activities. In later years, the Civil Service Commission established regional training centers and created the Federal Executive Institute in Charlottesville, Virginia, to provide executive development opportunities for senior managers in the classified service.

Many federal agencies now provide in-house training opportunities for their employees; some, such as the Social Security Administration and the Internal Revenue Service, have created large and well-staffed training centers. Still another training option pursued by some organizations is training provided by colleges and universities. Nonetheless, the total percentage of the personnel budget devoted to training remains small; in times of budgetary stress, training and development are always the first items to be cut. The federal government did not even have a government-wide training strategy until 1989, more than a hundred years after the creation of the merit system.

The Volcker Commission's Task Force on Education and Training reported in 1989 that, with a handful of exceptions, federal training is short-term in its focus, duration and effects. Although training "instances" doubled between fiscal year 1975 and fiscal year 1985, this growth was accomplished without increasing the real dollars spent on training. . . . Federal expenditures on training are absurdly low, if training is understood to be an element of investment for growth and productivity. The federal government spends about three-quarters of 1 percent of its payroll dollars on training. In contrast, many of the top-rated companies spend as much as 10 percent of payroll for this purpose, while the military devotes as much as 15 to 20 percent of its payroll dollars to this goal.[35]

Why does this matter? Because the federal government recruits specialists, rewards and promotes largely for technical and program expertise, and creates a career development path that is like a stovepipe in its narrowness and rigidity. These emphases, combined with limited training for those inside public organizations who are or will be managers, has important negative implications for management. Outstanding computer specialists or accountants are not necessarily good managers, and in the absence of substantial managerial education and training are not likely to be.

There are equally important implications for nonmanagerial personnel. The classification system has created narrow job descriptions and career paths. Career civil servants have little opportunity and few incentives to broaden their knowledge base or their skills and expertise. As knowledge and technology grow and change at an unprecedented pace, the need for constant reeducation and creation of problem-solving skills is great. Donald Kettl summarizes the issue: "Effective learning—indeed, effective public management—requires organizations [and their employees] to look past their internal operations, to gauge what is happening in the broader environment, to estimate the implications of these events for the organization's mission, and to adapt to those new challenges."[36]

All these issues are important for the contemporary merit system. David Rosenbloom and I argue that "merit and competence are inextricably intertwined."[37] Competence is, however, being redefined almost constantly. Education and training will have to be a more integral part of any future merit system than they have been historically.

Performance and Productivity

A final significant add-on is those efforts directed toward improving the productivity of government employees and measuring their performance. Again, the history is long but the products are meager. Scientific management's emphasis on efficiency and economy stimulated the first formal actions and the first definition of administrative efficiency: maximum output for minimum resource expenditure.

The 1910 Taft Commission (the Commission on Economy and Efficiency) recommended the creation of a Bureau of Efficiency within the Civil Service Commission. That bureau was created in 1916; its job was to create standards for efficiency that could be applied to all government employees. An underlying rationale for the passage of the Classification Act of 1923 was to improve efficiency and productivity. The Brownlow committee report spoke of "canons of efficiency," but moved away from individual productivity to argue for improved management capability and better mechanisms for executive control.

The Performance Appraisal Act of 1951 again emphasized individual performance. It included provisions for an annual appraisal and rating of each employee and stated that performance should be directly linked to both pay increases and promotion. This remained essentially a paper exercise, however, and had little effect on the increasingly common practice of promotion for tenure or time in place, rather than performance or productivity.

The most important additions to the system in terms of performance are the performance-appraisal and pay-for-performance provisions of the CSRA. Under these provisions, midlevel and senior managers continue to receive a set base pay, but are eligible for additional financial bonuses linked to an appraisal and rating of their individual performance. Public productivity and efficiency have become increasingly central as the cost of government (much of which is payroll) has become ever larger and as budget and economic constraints have increased.

Conclusion

The intent of this chapter is not to provide a comprehensive list of all the changes to the core civil service system that have occurred in the past forty years. Rather, it is to describe major additions to the system and to emphasize the almost haphazard way they have been grafted onto old provisions and processes. By the 1970s, the lack of internal consistency in the merit system, as well as the procedural baggage it had accumulated in the first hundred years of its history, created a system that was widely perceived to be broken.

In his campaign for the presidency in 1976, Jimmy Carter noted frequently that "there is no merit in the merit system." He proposed, not additional incremental change, but a comprehensive overhaul of merit.

That reform, the Civil Service Reform Act of 1978, was the first major reform of the system in nearly a hundred years. It was important in several respects: it provided a serious analysis of the state of merit; it examined the implications of the personnel system for effective management; and it represented the first significant presidential attention to civil service and merit issues since the administration of Theodore Roosevelt. The act—its design, provisions, and implementation experience—is described in the next chapter.

It is important to place the CSRA in the context of the overwhelming dissatisfaction with government and with the civil service that had emerged by the 1970s. There was a widespread perception that the War on Poverty and related efforts had failed; for many the war in Vietnam created a profound distrust of government generally. Watergate did nothing to reverse that.

Carter's efforts to redesign the civil service did not proceed with a clear view of what a civil service should be; with rare exceptions, the vision embodied in the CSRA combined a technical-efficiency perspective reminiscent of scientific management with a presidential-direction objective that sounded a lot like that of the Brownlow committee. Although it was clear that the existing system did not meet the needs and demands of modern government, it was much less obvious what those needs were—what government *should* be doing—and what the components of a system that addressed them would be. How or if such a civil service would emerge from a political system still concerned with control continued to be a significant, but little-discussed, part of the equation.

Chapter Five

Reforming

the System

The disjointed growth of the merit system and the gradual, but consistent, accretion of rules and regulations created a classified civil service system of enormous complexity. The "baggage" of merit went far beyond the fundamental merit principles; it contained regulations covering every possible aspect of personnel administration. Indeed, the merit principles themselves grew over the years. From the initial three included in the Pendleton Act, the principles grew to six in the Intergovernmental Personnel Act of 1970 (which also extended them to state and local governments) and to nine in the Civil Service Reform Act of 1978. The principles now reflect the tensions inherent in the jerry-built system. Efficiency is a formal principle; so, too, are workforce diversity, protection of whistle-blowers, performance appraisal and reward, and concern for the public interest.[1] David Rosenbloom and I observe that the principles are now "more comprehensive, but they are much, much more confusing."[2]

Other components of the system became equally troublesome. The complicated personnel procedures and regulations had become the world of personnel specialists; they, and the human-resource function they controlled, were increasingly removed from managers and management. In a report titled *Managers and Their Overburdened Systems,* the National Academy of Public Administration argued that complex regulations and red tape related to personnel, budgeting, financial management, accounting procedures, and information mandates had created a managerial climate that was punitive, negative, and so constraining that managers struggled against nearly insurmountable odds to be effective.[3]

These problems highlight the difficulties created by the long-term emphasis on *administering* procedures, rather than *managing* people and programs. Good management was not prized by the system; James Q. Wilson observes that "there are few rewards for being known as a good manager."[4] In the context of increasing dissatisfaction with public performance, however, the differences between management and administration became more important. Management was the creative and effective use of human resources. It was found, many dissatisfied observers argued, in the private sector. Administration was the application of rules and regulations. It was found, they said, in government. The fundamental problem was that the civil service system created administrators. Nothing about it facilitated or supported the individual authority, flexibility, or discretion increasingly identified with "excellent" management.

The ability of the government and its employees to respond to new directions and policies was questioned; both the organizations and the employees were perceived to be rigid and rooted in the past. Presidents became more concerned about their ability to manage and direct government organizations. The public was concerned about the increasing size and cost of government. At the same time, the power continually accruing to bureaucracy and bureaucratic actors in policy design and formulation, as well as in service delivery, was a growing issue.[5] The legitimacy of this role was questioned; lack of bureaucratic accountability was perceived to be a major influence on the problems government was experiencing. Both Congress and the president responded with additional efforts to exert controls from the top down.[6]

Clearly, some government organizations had become too large and too unwieldy. Merit and the civil service system were a significant part of the problem, but certainly were not the sole cause. A budget system that did not link personnel to program or service-delivery activity, for example, and set employment ceilings in isolation from other budgetary considerations, contributed to fragmentation and a lack of accountability, and to a lack of understanding. A poll conducted by the Roper Organization in 1978 and frequently cited to justify the need for reform found that only 10 percent of the citizens responding believed that government was free of corruption. Less than a fourth believed that government was an exciting place to work, and only 18 percent believed that government attracted the best people.[7]

The venerable Civil Service Commission itself had also become a problem. The commission had always served a dual function: it administered and protected the merit system, but it also advised and assisted the president in patronage matters. John Macy, the chair of the commission under the Johnson administration, argued that this was no problem, since he advised the president in the morning and administered the merit system in the afternoon. Others, however, were not so convinced. Particularly after the Watergate scandals, concerns about the clarity of the line between politics and merit became more pronounced.

Jimmy Carter's Reform: The Civil Service Reform Act of 1978

Jimmy Carter seized on the issue of civil service reform in the earliest stages of his campaign for president. His tenure as governor of Georgia had demonstrated not only the need for, but the potential of, reform. He believed that the lessons he had learned in Georgia could be transferred to the federal government and its bureaucracy, which he constantly referred to as the "giant Washington marshmallow." A primary architect of the reform, Jule Sugarman, drafted position papers outlining the major problems and probable solutions in Atlanta before Carter even hit the national campaign trail.[8]

Following his election, waged in large part on the premise of "fixing what's wrong with government," Carter appointed two major groups to pursue reform. The President's Reorganization Project had the imprimatur of the president's attention (he was the chair of the executive committee) and priority. The president's Personnel Management Project (PMP) had primary responsibility for preparing the civil service component of the reforms. A serious effort was made to elicit diverse perspectives on both the problems and the proposed solutions. Although the PMP was staffed largely by civil servants, the views of academic experts, private-sector leaders, members of labor unions, and citizen representatives were solicited in public hearings and other forums. Not surprisingly, both the problem statements and the solutions proved to be wide-ranging and sometimes contradictory.

This was partially due to the nature of the beast; the civil service system is arcane. Carter himself proclaimed it to be "eye glazing." Each group in the PMP addressed only a limited section of the system—for example, labor/management relations. Despite Carter's wish to focus in a comprehensive way on improved *management* of government programs, this approach and the sum of the many parts did not necessarily have that emphasis.

In addition, to attract broader public interest, rhetoric about the reform quickly took on rather inflammatory tones. Carter's "giant Washington marshmallow" theme, his promise to clear the deadwood from the bureaucracy (this referred to the well-known difficulty of firing civil servants with permanent status), and the consistent emphasis on increased whistle-blowing to weed out fraud and abuse all contributed to the perception that the reforms would have to be forced onto an unrepentant bureaucracy. This produced a peculiar circumstance: the members of the civil service being attacked in the selling of reform were the same people who would be revitalized public servants once the reforms were in place. Reforms aimed at whipping the civil service into shape, however, were not the same as those that would improve its management capabilities and productivity.

Further, the politics-administration relationship was being redefined again. Only a short time after Watergate, government (or the bureaucracy) was being described as the problem; stronger political direction was the solution to better government. For many in the classified service, both the political rhetoric and the politics of some of the solutions were problematic. A survey of members of the career civil service at about this time found not only that they did not believe the problems to be so severe as did the general population (although they clearly recognized problems), but that they considered some of the proposed reforms to be a "repoliticization" of the civil service.[9] This was reflected in the deliberations of the PMP:

> For the career bureaucrats involved in design, effective government was defined by the presence of a strong and neutral merit system to offset political extremism. President Carter, while abhorring the illegal activities of the Nixon administration, was more impressed by the need for the president to exert greater control over executive agencies than by the need to strengthen merit. His observation that there was no merit in the merit system did not suggest that he would consider strengthening it as a building block of the reform.[10]

The design of the reform, because of both the process and the political setting in which it occurred, could not be the rational activity Carter had initially envisioned. Although the chair of the PMP later declared that the deliberations of that group had been devoid of political pressures,[11] the conflicting views presented to it and the need to reconcile the demands of good management with those of improved political responsiveness presented a real need for compromise. The package that emerged reflected these tensions; the Civil Service Reform Act embodied the conflicts between politics and merit that characterized the one hundred years of history preceding the reform. The act proposed major changes in the merit system. To a considerable extent, those changes contained the seeds of the problems that the reformed system confronts today.

Contents of the Reform

The reform package had two major parts: the Civil Service Reform Act of 1978 and Reorganization Plan Number 2. The Reorganization Plan affected the *structure* of the merit system. It abolished the Civil Service Commission and replaced it with two new organizations. The Office of Personnel Management was to be responsible for human-resource planning for the federal government and management and agency advisory functions. The OPM was viewed as a monitoring and advisory agency, rather than as an administrator of personnel policies. The new office was given substantial powers of delegation to accomplish this end. The director of the OPM was to be a presidential appointee.

This redefinition of the role of the central personnel agency was significant. In terms of human-resource management, the creation of the OPM marked a turning away from the "policing" function of the Civil Service Commission to a more proactive planning and support function. In political terms, the president's power to appoint the director of the agency profoundly altered the politics/merit equation. This ability, combined with the president's other political appointment authority, absolutely ensured that the central personnel agency would be more responsive to political direction and control. For the human-resource potential of the OPM to be exploited, political support for it had to be in place both in the White House and in the organization's top office.

The second agency created was the Merit Systems Protection Board (MSPB). Its function was to oversee and safeguard merit and to hear employee appeals. Within the Merit Systems Protection Board, the Office of Special Counsel (OSC) was to investigate claims of abuse and prohibited practices and to provide additional appeals and protections for whistle-blowers.[12] The Merit Systems Protection Board was to be a three-member bipartisan board; it was given new powers of subpoena, the power to initiate disciplinary action, and the power to impose fines. A third new agency, the Federal Labor Relations Authority (FLRA), was created by Title VII of the Civil Service Reform Act. The part of the act creating the FLRA was submitted to Congress several weeks after the act's other components.

The Civil Service Reform Act itself had the following major components:

The Senior Executive Service

The Senior Executive Service was intended to clarify the policy role of the highest-ranking career members of the civil service and to replace their pay system with one that had a significant performance-based component. This part of the reform had been recommended several times before; a similar proposal was contained in the second Hoover Commission report and was proposed again during the Nixon administration. It spoke to the longstanding issue of the relationship between political appointees and career executives. James Pfiffner notes:

> The balance between presidential appointees and career executives in governing the United States is a fundamental question of who shall rule. But it is also a question of governmental and organizational mechanics. The democratic principle that the president along with political appointees ought to direct policy in the executive branch is not in question, but judgments about the most effective way to organize that control have been changing.[13]

The Civil Service Reform Act provided that members of the civil service in grades GS16–18 and executive service levels IV and V would essentially leave the classified service and enter the Senior Executive Service through individual contracts between the employee and the agency. The members would agree to be more mobile, transferring their management skills and expertise to other programs and even other agencies if their political supervisors deemed that appropriate. In return, members of the SES would be eligible to compete for financial bonuses and incentives. There were two levels of awards: performance awards at the agency level and Presidential Rank Awards. These latter awards could be either Meritorious Awards (up to ten thousand dollars) or Distinguished Awards (up to twenty thousand dollars). The legislation provided that 50 percent of the members of the SES in each agency could be eligible for bonuses annually and no more than 1 percent could receive Distinguished Awards.

The financial incentives were an important part of the SES package. From a management point of view, they were expected to increase individual productivity by motivating managers to pursue program and agency goals more actively. From the personal perspective of the members, the incentives were a way to escape the pay cap that had been created by the link between executive pay and that of members of Congress. For many potential members of the SES, that link created a top pay level that they had achieved rather early in their careers through rapid promotion. The pay link caused them to remain at the same level for several years and, conceivably, for the remainder of their federal careers. In addition, while the executives' salaries remained capped, the employees on their staff continued to receive promotions and increases, so that in many cases there was little difference between the salaries of the executives and the salaries of those they supervised. This resulted in problems of motivation and morale, but also created high expectations for the reform, since reform would provide the executives with the only way to escape the pay cap other than leaving government service. At the time of the reform in 1978, the level at the cap was about fifty-seven thousand dollars.

The SES title of the Civil Service Reform Act created a system that approximated the British "rank in person" system rejected by the earlier reformers. The new Senior Executive Service would contain six levels, and the personal qualifications and experience of a member, rather than the job description on which the old system relied, would determine where in those levels she would be placed. The level would determine base salary; success in obtaining financial rewards would determine total compensation. Awards of bonuses and other incentives would be based on an annual performance appraisal of each member of the Senior Executive Service. Those with the best ratings would be ranked by an agency-level Performance Review Board.

Another of the significant components of the SES reform was the explicit recognition of the policy role played by many potential members of the SES. In separating it from the classified service, the reform placed the Senior Executive Service in a kind of buffer zone between the merit employees and the political appointees in an organization. It is important to note, however, that it is possible to interpret this buffer quality, the mobility provisions, and the performance-award provisions of the SES as sign of increased political direction and control of the Senior Executive Service. Virtually all the decisions in this regard would be made by political appointees; as the top executives in the organization, they technically supervised the members of the SES. Further, the CSRA contained a provision that 10 percent of the membership of the Senior Executive Service could be political appointees. In practice, this would place political appointees among the members of the SES, as well as above them.[14]

The legislation also provided that members of the SES could be removed for poor performance. No member whose performance was rated less than fully successful was eligible for an award; a member who received an unsatisfactory rating could be transferred or removed from the SES. A member of the SES who received two unsatisfactory ratings in five years had to leave the SES, as did anyone who received two unsatisfactory ratings in consecutive years of any three-year period. Leaving the SES could either mean leaving federal service or accepting a demotion to

GS15. Other parts of the SES reform included provisions for additional education and career development and for sabbaticals from the agencies. These provisions were intended to improve the general management skills of the SES members.

In combination, these provisions described a dramatically different working environment for senior career executives. In some respects, the reforms tended to move them closer to the model of the elite British higher civil service; this is true of the "rank in person" and enhanced-policy-role components of the reform. In other respects, the reform moved career executives toward the American private-sector executive model of a proactive executive with adequate authority and discretion to manage the resources for which she was responsible. Other components of the reform moved the executives to a model of greater political responsiveness. The disjuncture between these was revealed in implementation.

Merit Pay

A pay-for-performance system for midlevel managers (GS and GM13–15) was also created by the Civil Service Reform Act. As with the pay-for-performance provisions for the Senior Executive Service, the intent of merit pay was to break the pattern of essentially automatic pay raises for midlevel employees. The merit-pay system was revenue neutral; that is, no additional funds were to be budgeted for it. Rather, the monies from all within-grade step increases for each designated work unit would be pooled to create a merit-pay "pot." Employees covered by merit pay would not receive step increases, nor would they receive their full comparability increases (they would receive only half). Any additional increases would have to come in the form of merit bonuses, the full amount of which would be added to base pay. The merit bonuses would be based on annual performance appraisals and ratings. Unsatisfactory and marginal employees would not receive any increases. The merit-pay plan was designed to become operative three years after passage of the legislation, so that other provisions of the reform, such as the SES, would be in place before merit-pay activities were undertaken.

Veterans' Preference

The legislation submitted to Congress proposed to curtail veterans' preference significantly. At the time of the reform, veterans' preference extended to entrance examinations, hiring, and reductions in force for an unlimited period. The reform proposed time limits on both hiring and reductions-in-force preference for nondisabled veterans, but did not change provisions for disabled veterans.

Protection of Whistle-blowers

The act created the Office of Special Counsel specifically to protect those federal employees who believed they had been victims of reprisal or other illegal treatment after they had revealed some wrongdoing on the part of their agency or its employees. To obtain the additional protections of the Office of Special Counsel, however, it was necessary for the employee to pursue all appeals procedures within the agency first.

Affirmative Action

Although it was expected that the reductions in veterans' preference would have a positive impact on the recruitment of women and minorities, the CSRA also contained language reaffirming the commitment to affirmative action. It did not, however, mandate any new programs or describe new responsibilities in this regard for the Office of Personnel Management.

Labor Relations and Collective Bargaining

As noted above, the labor-relations title of the Civil Service Reform Act was added after the main part of the legislation had been sent to Congress; the provisions were an effort to counter developing labor opposition to the legislation. The provisions have been described as "murky" and "confused"; one analysis reports that determining the intent of this title of the act "depends very much on whom you ask." [15] Newland describes the extensive role the unions themselves played in drafting that component of the legislation and in shepherding it through Congress. The need to compromise between the preferred labor positions and those initially taken by the Carter administration was the major influence on the final language and accounts for much of the lack of clarity. [16]

The labor-relations title of the CSRA proposed to place the federal labor-relations program on a statutory basis for the first time. In conjunction with the creation of the Federal Labor Relations Authority, this was a major step.

Research-and-Development Authority

Clearly recognizing that some of the proposed reforms were essentially experiments and had never been tried in the public sector, the legislation proposed to give new research-and-development authority to the Office of Personnel Management. Under this authority, the OPM would be able to contract for the conduct and evaluation of limited experiments with new approaches to personnel management in public organizations.

Passage of the Civil Service Reform Act

The Carter administration was generally pleased with the reform package. Alan K. (Scotty) Campbell, who would later be the first director of the Office of Personnel Management and who had been active in the reform process, provided this summary:

> Some have argued that to solve the problems associated with federal personnel management would require the addition of even more rules and regulations. One could envision a system in which every action could have a check and balance, and every decision a midlevel review. This might eradicate abuse, but it would also thwart productivity. A balance must be struck between the freedom necessary to service the public's needs and the oversight required to protect the system's integrity. The President's Reorganization Plan and the Civil Service Reform Act strike the appropriate and necessary balance. Their significance to the president demonstrates that personnel management has rightly taken its place among the top priorities of the federal government.[17]

The politics of passage and the language that surrounded the public selling of the reform, however, had a different emphasis. Arguing that civil service reform was not a "sexy issue," Campbell himself adopted a weed-out-inefficiency-and-mismanagement approach in public speeches and writings. President Carter tended to stress the difficulties in firing federal employees and the need to protect whistle-blowers who could expose waste, fraud, and abuse. As Chester Newland notes, "Two impressions were encouraged: that the federal government was full of non-performers, and that the civil service system protected these employees. . . . the negative image of civil service that resulted was one of the most powerful and enduring products of the politics of CSRA—but it helped to get the reform adopted."[18]

The legislation emerged from the Congress relatively intact, but with support that Campbell characterized as "a mile wide, but an inch deep."[19] Labor relations and veterans' preference were, as anticipated, the most controversial parts of the package, and in the final legislation, limitations on the hiring of veterans were eliminated except as they applied to those who retired at a rank above major. With the support of the federal-employee unions, a provision was added to the labor-relations title that permitted judicial review of orders issued by the Federal Labor Relations Authority. In the House of Representatives, a new affirmative-action program was added to the act. The Federal Equal Opportunity Recruitment Program was intended to encourage the active recruitment of minorities and women.[20] The Civil Service Reform Act was approved by Congress and signed by President Carter in October 1978. It was described as Jimmy Carter's most impressive domestic political victory.

The Reality of Implementation

In many respects, the implementation of the CSRA altered it more than had congressional consideration and compromise. There were two major kinds of changes influencing the early years of civil service reform. First, some provisions of the act itself were altered as implementation proceeded. In the cases of the Senior Executive Service and merit pay, the differences were significant and had a major impact. In other cases, such as the delegation of examining and other authorities to agencies outside the Office of Personnel Management, the changes were simply reversals of policy: delegate, recentralize, delegate, recentralize, and so on. The second major influence on implementation was the dramatic change in the political environment created by the election of Ronald Reagan in 1980. It is useful to consider each of these influences in turn.

The Process of Implementation

Initial implementation activities were swift and decisive. The Office of Personnel Management was quickly created; it inherited the physical facility, as well as most of the staff and other resources, of the old Civil Service Commission. Scotty Campbell and Jule Sugarman were named director and deputy director. As Carolyn Ban notes, "strong leadership with a clear sense of mission was in place, ready to move decisively on their agenda for the agency."[21] That basic agenda was, in Campbell's words, to create a system in which personnel managers were "a part of management, rather than either servants of management or policemen of the civil service system."[22] Campbell noted further that the OPM "would perform for the president the same role relative to personnel management that OMB (the Office of Management and Budget) does for financial management."[23]

The Merit Systems Protection Board was also quickly put in place, but the dual nature of its responsibility precluded an easy infancy. The precise nature of the relationship between the MSPB and the Office of Special Counsel, scarce resources, and the uncertain place of the MSPB in the new institutional scheme contributed to turbulent early years. In selling civil service reform, the Merit Systems Protection Board and the Office of Special Counsel had often been presented as designed to balance the new flexibilities contained in the act, particularly with reference to the SES and performance appraisal and pay.

In practice, this meant that the MSPB had oversight not only of the agencies, but of the Office of Personnel Management as well. The Office of Special Counsel was to be "an aggressive protector of merit systems principles and of employees harmed by prohibited personnel practices." [24] To accomplish these ends, the counsel was given specific tenure in office and considerable independence from the parent MSPB. In theory, this made good sense; in practice, it created an uncomfortable working relationship, which was exacerbated by a consistent failure to fund and staff the OSC fully.

While the relationships between the new institutions of reform were being worked out, a relatively long-term and decentralized implementation strategy for the rest of the reforms was being put in place. The OPM realized that not all federal agencies were equally interested in assuming, or willing or able to assume, responsibility for the reforms. The OPM itself had limited resources for the enormous implementation effort. Ban calls the task "staggering" and observes that nearly 130,000 managers and members of the Senior Executive Service needed to be educated about and trained for their new responsibilities. If pay for performance was to be effective, performance standards and appraisal systems had to be developed for a workforce of 2.3 million people.[25] Further, there were few, if any, public-sector models or examples to fall back on. Necessarily, the early stages of implementation were a learning exercise.

The Senior Executive Service

Other major components of the reform endured similar early experiences. The Senior Executive Service, considered by many the cornerstone of the reform because of its emphasis on improved and more-flexible management, encountered major changes in its first year. That first year also saw 98 percent of the 6,919 eligible employees opt to sign the SES contract. As the earlier discussion of pay caps and compression indicated, for many the SES was financially "the only game in town." This compensation issue framed, and probably distorted, expectations for the SES among its charter members. Neither the management emphasis nor the new flexibility nor the policy potential was frequently cited as an incentive to join. Against this background, the early changes take on special significance.

The legislation had passed with the provision that 50 percent of the executives in an agency could be eligible for a bonus in any year. The first agency to move through the process and to award bonuses was the National Aeronautics and Space Administration (NASA). It awarded bonuses to the full percentage permissible. Congress, which had paid little attention to the numbers in hearings on the bill, reacted angrily, indicating that 50 percent was an outside boundary, not a required level. Congress reduced the number of those eligible from 50 percent to 25 percent six months after the reform was put in place. The Office of Personnel Management, wishing to demonstrate its responsibility to Congress, used its rule-making authority to reduce eligibility to 20 percent. Campbell later said that the original 50 percent had been in the bill only to allow for compromise to a lower figure, which was always considered more appropriate. Because the little debate that did occur about the SES focused on other issues (for example, should it be a three-year experiment rather than a permanent institution?), the 50 percent figure was never challenged and the strategy backfired.[26] The change in the number of members eligible for bonuses had an immediate impact on the Senior Executive Service; many argued that it constituted a breach of their SES contracts.[27]

There was a significant exodus from the SES in the early years of its existence, and analysts suggest different reasons for it. Without any doubt, the bonus issue was a factor; so, too, was the politicization and bureaucrat bashing of the first Reagan administration. Some members of the Senior Executive Service left because they were close to retirement and were able to take advantage of favorable retirement-benefit calculations, while still others took better-paying jobs in the private sector.[28] In any case, over half of the charter members of the Senior Executive Service were no longer in government service three years later.

Other provisions of the SES reform were equally troublesome. Not many career members of the SES ascended to policymaking positions (fewer than twelve government wide in the first four years). The sabbatical program was not created until much later. The mobility provisions were widely perceived to be punitive, and a method to get rid of unwanted personnel, rather than as tools for improved management or career-development purposes. Few instances of abuse were documented, however.[29] More significantly, implementation clarified the faulty base of a critical assumption: senior managers in the American federal service were, and always had been, technical experts or program specialists. Although many of the members of the Senior Executive Service were excellent managers, they had risen through the career ranks on the basis of narrow program or technical skills, not on the basis of general management ability. Many of them had not, in fact, had managerial training before they received their first management positions, well into their federal careers. They were not, in short, the managerial generalists necessary for the mobility model; in that sense the reform could not work as designed.

Merit Pay

The merit-pay provisions of the Civil Service Reform Act became effective in October 1981. As Karen Gaertner and Gregory Gaertner observed, merit pay did not stand alone as a reform; its success was highly contingent on the effectiveness of the performance standards and performance-appraisal systems that had just been put in place in most agencies. Together, performance standards, performance appraisal, and merit pay created a dramatically different performance system in the federal service. But each had to be successful for the others to succeed.[30]

The initial success of merit pay was also linked closely to the revenue-neutral provisions of the legislation. Research on the issue of pay and motivation indicated two critical links. First, the employee had to perceive a clear and fair link between performance and award. In other words, the appraisal process had to be effective. Second, the employee had to value the award.[31] The limited funding permitted by the CSRA provisions cast some doubt on the availability of adequate resources; the implementation of merit pay government wide cast some doubt on the ability to train and educate people adequately for the appraisal process prior to its implementation.

Given the conditions for success, it is not surprising that merit pay did not meet them. There are many evaluations of the merit-pay reforms. Two summaries provide a good overview. The first, by researchers under contract to the OPM to study the CSRA's effectiveness, concludes that

> merit pay is not working in our two agencies or in most of the other agencies in which evaluations are taking place. By not working, we mean that it is not widely accepted, it is not seen as an improvement, it is not rewarding deserving people with significant raises, and it is not contributing to agency effectiveness. The second conclusion is that performance standards and performance appraisal may be working to improve the way in which employees are able to plan and accomplish their work goals.[32]

Another early evaluation funded by the Office of Personnel Management reached the same general conclusions; Jone Pearce, James Perry, and William Stevenson concluded that merit pay was not effective in the agencies they examined, either in terms of motivating individual employees for better performance or in terms of increasing organizational effectiveness.[33]

Three years after merit pay had first been implemented, Congress abolished it and replaced it with the Performance Management and Review System (PMRS). The new system was substantially different from merit pay. Using a five-level, standardized appraisal system, the PMRS provided that employees rated in the two levels above fully successful must receive the annual general or comparability increase, but could also compete for merit increases and be eligible for performance awards or bonuses. The new system was not revenue neutral, but agencies were limited to paying out 1.5 percent of payroll for performance awards.[34]

The overall record of the PMRS was similar to that of merit pay; there were few indications of clear success. It is important to note, however, that some agencies, such as the Internal Revenue Service and agencies at the Department of Defense, argued that their systems were generally satisfactory and functioned as effective management tools. Overall, the analyses of the PMRS indicated that there were fewer problems with linking appraisal to reward, but that problems with the size of the awards and their perceived adequacy still existed.[35]

In 1990, the Bush administration gave serious consideration to extending the pay-for-performance idea to all levels of the civil service throughout government, but its lack of success with programs in both the public and private sectors and significant opposition from employee unions caused the plan to be dropped.[36] A subsequent analysis of the feasibility of extension was created by a provision of the Federal Employee Pay Comparability Act of 1990. A joint labor-management committee again opposed the extension of pay for performance, arguing that limited experiments were necessary before expansion in a public setting could be considered.[37] In 1993, Congress abolished the PMRS.

Research and Development
Implementation of the research-and-development provisions of the CSRA has been relatively modest. A major demonstration project, commonly referred to as China Lake, was initiated shortly after passage of the legislation. The China Lake demonstration covers two naval research laboratories in California and includes about seventy-six hundred employees. It was initially intended to last for five years and to end in 1985; it was extended twice, however, and was slated to end in 1995. The demonstration has been extensively evaluated by the Office of Personnel Management; it is one of the best-documented experiments in public management.[38]

The China Lake demonstration project has three broad objectives: to create flexible management systems, to give managers more discretion in using those systems, and to reward employees who perform exceptionally well. The demonstration includes pay banding, which replaces rigid classification and compensation levels with broad pay bands linked to five general career paths: professional, technical, administrative, technical specialist, and clerical specialist. Starting salaries in each band are flexible; increases and bonuses are linked to performance appraisal and can be up to 10 percent of base pay. The appraisal system is less standardized and rigid than that used throughout the rest of the federal system. Both the general demonstration and the specific components were devised by navy personnel in conjunction with the staffs of the research laboratories.

The OPM has reported positive findings from the China Lake project. A ten-year evaluation reports that the perceived link between performance and pay has been substantially strengthened, that support for performance pay has grown, and that turnover among high performers has decreased.[39] Analyses from other sources are less sanguine. The U.S. General Accounting Office (GAO), an arm of Congress, reported, for example, that the China Lake demonstration has been expensive and has had access to financial resources that permitted salary increases of approximately 1 percent per year.[40] The GAO noted that this condition was unlikely to be replicated in other federal settings.

Other demonstration projects have targeted different issues. The Pacer Share demonstration, for example, was created by the air force and implemented at McClellan Air Force Base in California. Pacer Share covered about eighteen hundred employees, in both blue- and white-collar occupations. The primary objective of Pacer Share was to increase organizational effectiveness and productivity; to do so it used a group gainsharing plan. Cost savings at the end of each year were divided equally between the air force and the employees. Pacer Share also included a simplified classification system and a more flexible pay structure; it eliminated individual performance appraisals, replacing them with group goals and objectives. The demonstration was assembled with labor-management collaboration.

Pacer Share is difficult to evaluate because the demonstration site was the target of major budget and staff cuts while the demonstration was being implemented; in fact, it was recommended that all of McClellan Air Force Base be closed. Pacer Share has now been terminated. It is clear that the project did not achieve all that it intended: performance payments were much smaller than anticipated and there was no evidence that overall costs were reduced. Average salaries, in fact, increased.[41]

The final demonstration that is of broad interest is that being conducted by the National Institute of Science and Technology (NIST). This project covers about three thousand employees; it was specifically designed to be budget neutral despite an emphasis on performance-related pay. The demonstration also includes simplified classification and recruitment arrangements, as well as bonuses to facilitate hiring and retention of critical scientific and technical staff members. Implementation of the NIST demonstration was rather turbulent because of opposition to the demonstration within NIST's parent agency and initial opposition from the Office of Personnel Management. Some changes were made in the design of the demonstration in its second year. The OPM's assessment of the project was that there appeared to be increasing employee acceptance of the experiment, but it was not possible to draw clear conclusions about the program's overall effectiveness.

Despite some negative evaluations, the personnel and management reforms suggested by the demonstration projects have had a relatively broad impact. In 1986, the Civil Service Simplification Act was submitted to Congress with the support of the OPM. That legislation would have created broad bands of occupations and pay in a limited number of federal agencies; all others would have continued to operate within the existing civil service system. The bill did not pass, but the issue of classification reform has become a part of the agenda for public management reform, with some leading authorities, such as the National Academy of Public Administration, recommending fundamental change.[42]

The Office of Personnel Management has carefully analyzed the results of the demonstrations with an eye to the design of future reforms and to the kinds of organizations in which more-flexible systems are most likely to be effective.[43] The data created by the research and demonstration provisions of the CSRA should have a major impact on the next generation of reforms; many of the demonstration activities, such as broad-banding, were included in the recommendations of the National Performance Review.

Political Influences on Civil Service Reform

Some of the implementation history of the Civil Service Reform Act reflected flaws in design and a failure to provide adequate resources; a major part of that history is also related to the political environment in which the reforms occurred. Jimmy Carter was clearly committed to the CSRA. The implementation plan for the legislation was consciously long-term and recognized the difficulties of major organizational and individual change. The phasing in of merit pay three years after passage of the bill, for example, anticipated that the Senior Executive Service would be implemented and institutionalized, that performance standards and appraisal systems would be created, and that merit pay could build on this base.

In fact, however, the election of Ronald Reagan in 1980 so profoundly changed the political climate in which federal agencies operated that the base did not exist. The presidential transition and the bureaucrat-bashing tone that characterized it created a period of "stressful change" for federal organizations.[44] The career civil servants who were both the targets of the reform changes and the implementors of those changes were also the targets of strongly antibureaucratic rhetoric. President Reagan asserted that government is "not the solution to the problem. Government *is* the problem"; this did not suggest that strong relationships would develop between the president and the civil service. The budget cuts and staff reductions in the first Reagan term further destabilized the environment of federal organizations. For civil service reform, the political changes were overwhelming.

The changing environment was clearly evident at the Office of Personnel Management. Scotty Campbell, one of the reform's designers and strong supporters, was replaced as the director of the OPM by Donald Devine, a former political operative in the Reagan campaign. Devine reduced the agency's budget, staff, and mission. He described the OPM as a political actor and its primary function as that of a key advisor to the president on political management.[45] Larry Lane observes, "The major focus of Devine's agenda was to replace OPM's traditional management orientation with an unswerving emphasis on responsiveness of the public service solely to political direction from within the executive branch." [46]

Even though later directors of the OPM attempted to move the organization back toward a more positive role, the experience in the early Reagan years came at a critical time in the shaping of the reform. Several outcomes were evident. First, the vitally important relationship between the SES and political executives did not develop, except in negative terms. Devine and other appointees created a combat zone, not a place to build new partnerships, assume more discretion, and emphasize good management.

The long-term tension between politics and the civil service was again the defining characteristic of the relationship; not only were the reforms overwhelmed by the political turbulence, but any positive role the civil service and its senior managers could play was cast aside. The conundrum of bureaucratic power was addressed in classic scientific-management terms: political executives give the directions and career executives, as John Ehrlichman put it, jump. The difference from the earlier version was that bureaucratic power was now a force to be controlled; bureaucratic expertise was not considered an asset, but an obstacle to the achievement of presidential policy priorities.

At a time when the United States had an opportunity to use components of the Civil Service Reform Act to rebuild a system in serious disrepair and to focus the energies of the career civil service in a more positive way, another road was taken. The civil service and the federal government were again confronted with their historical dilemmas: the "proper" role of politics and the public service; the relationship between political appointees and career executives; the hiring of senior civil servants who have the flexibility, discretion, and authority to be managers, rather than appliers of rules; and, once again, the role of bureaucratic authority and power in a democratic system.

This provides remarkable contemporary evidence of the continuing connections among the public service, politics, and political movements. The "Reagan revolution" was an attack on both the quality and the size of government; it reflected widespread citizen dissatisfaction. Because government was the problem, its employees could not be part of the solution. The need to establish the fundamental legitimacy of the public service and its power was once again a primary issue.

Chapter Six

Presidential

Management

Strategies

Political Executives and the

Higher Civil Service

The merit system is a product of, and is inextricably related to, politics and the political environment. Nonetheless, it has frequently been perceived, described, and reformed as if it were a mechanistic apparatus, isolated and insulated from the realities of the world of politics. Additions and reforms have had a technical tone, reflecting the themes of economy and efficiency prevalent in the earlier part of this century. At the same time, however, another important pattern has been present. At least from the time of the Brownlow committee, there have been consistent efforts by presidents to achieve more-effective control of the civil service. These reforms, though sometimes also couched in technical terms, have reflected a much broader theme: governance and the proper role of a permanent civil service in a democratic society. These presidential management reforms are basically about power: the power of the permanent bureaucracy, the power of the president in relation to that bureaucracy, and (occasionally) the power of Congress in relation to both.

The role that the Brownlow committee report defined for the president was that of chief executive officer of the executive branch. The committee's argument that, as a responsible chief executive, the president should be "the center of energy, direction and administrative management"[1] for the federal government assumed a managerial capacity that did not exist in the executive office of the president at the time. Many would argue that it still does not. Every president since Franklin Roosevelt, however, has had a strategy, or set of strategies, for improving presidential control of the civil service and for becoming that "center of energy."

The primary value underpinning these strategies is not economy or efficiency, but responsiveness. Responsiveness in this context means being responsive to the president's goals and policies, rather than to the many other influences that operate in contemporary politics. Herbert Kaufman argues that the interplay of these values—efficiency, effectiveness, and responsiveness—should be seen as a cycle, with one ascending while the others descend. All are consistently present in the American system, he says, but all do not have equal power at any given time.[2]

Recent efforts to improve responsiveness have not been so inclusive, however. The president has been seen as the primary actor; lines of authority have run directly from the president and his agents to the bureaucracy. Not surprisingly, most of the strategies for presidential management that arise from this view are based on a simple hierarchical model that is essentially Weberian in its assumptions. This model was summarized succinctly by Donald Devine: "The skill and technical expertise of the career service must be utilized, but it must be utilized under the direct authority and personal supervision of the political leader who has the moral authority flowing from the people through an election."[3]

This view of responsiveness is too simplistic in two ways. The perception of the civil service as a tidy, easily managed set of structures is not accurate. Neither is the view of the clarity of the managerial authority and ability of the president and his appointees. Nonetheless, the presidential-control model has had an important influence on the civil service in the past fifty years.

Two qualities of this set of reforms bear comment. First, the reforms are generally part of a larger set of activities that include structural reorganization, budgetary reductions and changes, and policy reconfiguration. Controlling the bureaucracy is critical to achieving the larger policy objectives. Second, to the extent that these reforms emphasize *presidential* management and bureaucratic responsiveness to presidential directives, they necessarily deemphasize managerial flexibility and discretion in the civil service itself. They are based on the neutral competence model of the scientific-management theorists and on the simple and routine qualities of public management that those theorists assumed. The next chapter will examine the changing nature of public work and management; this chapter will focus on presidential management strategies and their fit with the reality of the merit system.

The Problem of Bureaucratic Control

The growth in the size, complexity, and influence of public bureaucracies and the civil service employees who staff and manage them is an issue of serious concern for modern government. At the same time that the civil service has become overwhelming in its complexity, the functions performed by its members, and the need to carry them out effectively and efficiently, have become ever more fundamental to good government.

Further, organizations structured for stability and standardization are now called upon to be innovative, flexible, and entrepreneurial. The need for organizations to change in response to presidential elections, congressional and judicial mandates and directives, new knowledge, new problems, and more-limited resources is nearly constant. But how to direct and control these changes? Mosher's question is again appropriate: "How can a public service so constituted be made to operate in a manner compatible with democracy?"[4]

There are at least four important parts to this question. The first is how to define and delineate the legitimate role of public bureaucracy in the public policy process. The realities of modern government have overshadowed the simple clarity of the politics-administration dichotomy and the neutral, competent administrator.[5] Suitable replacements, however, have not been found.

The second major issue is the relationship of the president and his staff to the bureaucracy, in terms of both policy direction and management. The first and second issues are closely related because, as the Devine statement quoted above indicates, much of the rationale for contemporary presidential management strategies relies on outdated concepts that have limited relevance for contemporary government, policy, and management.

The third issue is the role of Congress. Given the concern at the time of the passage of the Pendleton Act that creation of a strong central personnel system could be unconstitutional because it involved tipping the balance of power, what role should Congress play in maintaining its authority in light of management strategies based on unilateral presidential authority?

The fourth issue is the tension between bureaucratic institutions and democratic governance. Although not all government organizations are bureaucracies, the standardization and rigidity of the civil service system have created bureaucratic characteristics in many of them. This is significant because, while bureaucracies are well suited for some tasks and functions, there are other things they do not do well. Bureaucratic organizations and the rules and routines they create are good at standardized, routine, predictable behavior. One of the things they are not good at is change. Change can and does occur in large bureaucratic organizations, but it is long-term and generally slow. The power of routine and the weight of regulations can stultify and overwhelm change, no matter how important or carefully planned. This is not the fault of the organizations and their employees; it is a result of the structure of the organization and its purpose: to maintain stability and predictability.

The electoral system, on the other hand, permits citizens to introduce change into the system based on shifting preferences, values, and political choices. Furthermore, this change is frequent and potentially dramatic. Elected officials, particularly presidents, come to office with a brief window of opportunity to implement their policy agendas. They are watched closely by the media and by the electorate and are judged quickly for perceived success or failure. The rapt attention paid to a president's first hundred days is a case in point. If presidents are not able to show substantive results quickly, they are frustrated, and often on the defensive. The permanent bureaucracy is a frequent and convenient target for blame. The tensions in the system are described by Gregory Gaertner and Karen Gaertner's study of presidential transitions:

> In a basic sense, these contradictions suggest that the conditions for an effective democratic regime that responds quickly to shifting electoral mandates are not the conditions that support effective operation of the large organizations designed to implement that mandate . . . the contradiction is most forceful when the transition represents an extreme departure from established ways of doing business.[6]

Kaufman's cycle, therefore, is not benign. The shift from one value to another usually occurs because of dissatisfaction—often profound dissatisfaction—with the operation of the civil service and the permanent bureaucracy. The merit system represents an obstacle to change and an excuse for not changing. That is why merit is often not a high priority for presidents, or prominent in their management strategies. The fundamental values that presidents *do* prize were well summarized by President Nixon's director of personnel:

> In our constitutional form of government, the executive branch is, and always will be, a political institution. This is not to say that the application of good

management practices, sound policy formulation, and the highest calibre of program implementation are not of vital importance. The best politics is still good government. But you cannot achieve management, policy, or program control unless you have established political control.[7]

To achieve a better understanding of the implications of this commitment to political control, as well as the relevance of some of the components of the strategies for political management that presidents have devised, it is useful to examine the approaches of the presidents who have pursued their strategies most vigorously.

Presidential Management Strategies

Every president during this century has pursued some level of governmental reorganization or reform. The president has often relied on "blue ribbon" citizen committees to clarify the problems or ratify proposed solutions; there has been such a group or commission formed on an average of every seven years this century.[8] Franklin Roosevelt initially chose to bypass the merit system whenever possible. President Eisenhower created Schedule C appointments to increase his capacity for control. During the presidency of Richard Nixon, however, following the Great Society and the War in Vietnam, a comprehensive strategy emerged.

The Administrative Presidency

Richard Nixon came to office convinced that the permanent bureaucracy was populated by staff members antagonistic to his policy priorities. There is some empirical evidence that he was correct. Joel Aberbach and Bert Rockman, for example, found that, in some agencies, permanent staffers remained strongly committed to the Great Society initiatives of the Johnson administration.[9] This is in keeping with other research, which has found strong ties to programs and policies among members of the career civil service.[10] It is also in keeping with the impact of the classification system on the civil service, which recruits and hires for program or professional expertise and promotes for program skills until midlevel management positions are achieved.[11] After people have served one program or policy for a long time, some attachments to that program or policy are inevitable; one senior executive observed that asking career members to change "their" programs and policies drastically was a bit like asking them "to kill their children."[12]

These are precisely the ties, however, that presidential management strategies are intended to sever. Nixon set about doing so by using a multipronged strategy, the foundation of which was the Ash Council.

The Ash Council was created in 1969 and chaired by Roy Ash, the president of Litton Industries. Although President Nixon argued that the problems with the executive branch were "principally a matter of machinery," [13] he asked the council for a comprehensive analysis of the entire executive branch and promised to "change the framework of government itself." [14]

The recommendations of the council were sweeping, but two are of particular relevance here. First, the council focused on structural changes that would strengthen the managerial capacity of the executive office of the president. This included creating the Office of Management and Budget to replace the Bureau of the Budget, creating the Domestic Council, and reorganizing the agencies in the executive branch into four "superdepartments." [15]

The reorganization effort was to be accompanied by programmatic changes that would replace fragmented categorical programs with much broader block grants. The intent of all these changes was to increase policy direction and coordination and to provide the president with a staff to oversee the changes.

Second, and significantly for the merit system, the Ash Council recommendations focused on using political appointees to oversee and supplement the structural changes. These recommendations reflected the fundamental distrust of the career civil service noted above. To some extent, they also reflected President Nixon's distrust of his own cabinet. The problem of "not cav[ing] in to the bureaucrats," in Nixon's term, or "marrying the natives," in John Ehrlichman's term, was a consistent issue for the president and his top staff members.[16] They did not believe they could maintain control of top political appointees once those appointees became enmeshed in the organizations they were sent to direct. It was necessary, therefore, to add appointees who could screen bureaucratic influences and maintain presidential policy objectives. This increased use of political appointments, based on a fundamental distrust of the career civil service, was to become a cornerstone of Nixon's management efforts. It was also to become a part of the strategy of every president who followed him.

Congress was not receptive to many components of the Nixon strategy. Just as members of an earlier Congress had looked with great skepticism on the recommendations from the Brownlow committee that were advanced by Franklin Roosevelt, members of this Congress would not approve measures that would strengthen the presidency at their expense.

Additional efforts were then made by the White House. At the end of Nixon's first term, the impounding of funds approved by Congress for domestic programs—particularly the remnants of Great Society programs—had become a part of the strategy. Extensive use of political appointees and a political-clearance process for merit appointments was also key.[17] James Pfiffner notes that the excesses of the Nixon strategy resulted from a lack of "constitutional tradition" among his top staffers. They believed, he argues, that "the president had the sole right and duty to run the government."[18] This belief was manifest in Watergate; the events surrounding that debacle effectively ended the Nixon management strategy, as well as the Nixon presidency. The lessons of the Nixon effort, however, were quickly picked up by succeeding presidents.

The Technical Presidency

Although Jimmy Carter's Civil Service Reform Act was discussed in some detail in chapter 5, other elements of his presidential management strategy also deserve discussion. First, it is important to note that civil service reform was part of a larger effort called the President's Reorganization Project. Carter, too, wanted to reorganize to improve presidential control. The structural changes in the federal personnel system that were achieved through Reorganization Plan Number 2 and the CSRA also served to clarify presidential direction. Quite clearly, having a single director of the Office of Personnel Management appointed by the president improved presidential control of that agency.

Other Carter reorganization initiatives were not so successful. In his campaign, he promised to reduce the number of federal agencies from nineteen hundred to two hundred. Although ten of the eleven reorganization plans he submitted were approved, he did not meet his campaign target.[19]

Carter had, however, learned several lessons from the Nixon experience. While he did not wish to replicate the abuses of the merit system, Carter's rhetoric indicated quite strongly that he did not consider the civil service an ally in his efforts to improve government. The newly created Senior Executive Service gave Carter an instrument that Nixon did not have. (The Nixon proposal for a Federal Executive Service had not been passed by Congress.) Carter's reform lacked the punitive language in that proposed by President Nixon and it reduced the total number of members who could be political appointees, but it achieved the same general purpose.[20] The ability to place some political appointees throughout the bureaucracy, rather than only in top-level, policy-sensitive positions, provided the president with an opportunity to reach further into the agencies for control purposes. The mobility provisions of the SES, while technically meant to provide for broader career development for the career managers, also gave top political executives the opportunity to move career managers they did not want to work with and to remove potential sources of opposition to the changes they proposed.

President Carter also availed himself of a political initiative that Richard Nixon had not used: the increased use of Schedule C appointees. Where Nixon had turned to illegal manipulation of the merit system to increase the numbers of employees he deemed appropriately loyal, Carter turned to the policy-sensitive appointment system created by President Eisenhower. Until this time, Schedule Cs had made up a relatively small part of the total presidential appointments. Further, they had been largely in lower-level appointments: confidential secretaries and assistants, chauffeurs, and aides. The Carter administration not only increased the total numbers; it increased them at the GS13–15 level, which involved mid- to upper-level management. At the end of the Ford administration, there were 911 Schedule C appointments government wide. At the end of the Carter administration, there were 1,566, of which 855 were at the GS13–15 level.

Carter combined this increased politicization with a firm belief in technical controls. The systems for performance appraisal and reward contained in the Civil Service Reform Act are one excellent example: formal, standardized processes were created for monitoring, evaluating, and rewarding or punishing employee performance.[21] Even the technical efforts have a political side, however, particularly for the Senior Executive Service, because the executives evaluating members of the SES are political appointees. Other provisions of the SES reinforce this influence. Its members may be demoted by being shifted to much less responsible positions; they can be removed from the SES if they receive unsatisfactory performance ratings. In combination with larger numbers of midlevel political appointees, the technical provisions of the SES permit its members to be excluded from decision making and, for some, from managerial responsibilities as well.

Other technical reforms from the Carter years, such as zero-based budgeting and clearer financial controls, also served to increase presidential influence inside federal agencies, thereby clarifying how external control could be enhanced. Obviously, such reforms can serve the purposes of better management and better political direction. In the case of the Nixon administration, efforts at better political control crossed the line between responsiveness and illegal political activity. In the case of the Carter administration, increased efforts at political management were accompanied by efforts to improve the technical efficiency of the huge government apparatus. In neither case did the strategy achieve the intended outcome. That did not deter the next president, Ronald Reagan, from elaborating the strategy still further.

The Politicized Presidency

Terry Moe labeled the Reagan administration's approach to managing the bureaucracy "the politicized presidency," arguing that ideological politics played a key role in the strategy.[22] This differed sharply from the previous efforts, which one analyst described in this way: "The political personnel system creates what is basically an accidental collection of individuals with little past commitment to political leadership and few enduring stakes in government's own capabilities and performance."[23] Ronald Reagan's most important contribution to presidential management strategies was that the political executives he appointed did not fit that description. The Reagan transition personnel staff had a hundred members; it was at least triple the size of previous transition staffs. One student of presidential transitions argues that the Reagan effort was the best funded, the most focused, and the most intensive in the postwar period, and possibly ever.[24] The effort was not only intensive, but notable for the extent to which partisan and ideological clearance processes were used. These clearance procedures were also applied to larger numbers of political appointees than before; close attention was paid to Schedule Cs. Although these clearances slowed the process down, they were intended to ensure that Reagan appointees had a sure sense of mission, and that policy initiatives would not be distorted once the appointees were inside the bureaucracy.

The Reagan strategy and policy priorities were clearly spelled out by the Heritage Foundation, a conservative policy institute, in its publication *Mandate for Leadership*. To some extent, the Heritage recommendations broke from the traditional hierarchical models of presidential direction and control by advocating that career staff simply be bypassed whenever possible.[25] In addition, in some agencies, particularly central management agencies such as the Office of Personnel Management and the Office of Management and Budget, there was an effort to employ what Reagan strategists called "jigsaw puzzle management."[26] That strategy was to create new decision-making networks in the organization by placing political appointees in critical points throughout the organization, thereby excluding career managers not only from policy decisions but from most policy information. The term was coined because the strategists believed that only political managers should understand how all the pieces of the policy puzzle fit together; career civil servants should not be privy to such information. Chester Newland describes these early activities: "The focus was on confident and decisive change—implementing a fixed idea of governance—to the neglect of matters of longer term success, including management."[27]

There was also an effort to target agencies whose policy mandate was not favored in the Reagan presidency. Thus, the number of Schedule C appointments at the GS13–15 levels tripled from 1976 to 1986 in the Departments of Labor, the Interior, and Health and Human Services, and more than doubled at Housing and Urban Development and Agriculture. The Department of Education, created during the Carter presidency, had seventy-four Schedule Cs at the GS13–15 level by 1986.[28] Although some of this increase occurred during the Carter administration, the Reagan strategy raised the total at the GS13–15 levels and also raised the number of appointees in the central management agencies. At the Office of Management and Budget, the Office of Personnel Management, the Merit Systems Protection Board, and the General Services Administration, for example, the number of political appointees increased by almost 50 percent during the first Reagan term. In the same period, the total number of career staff members in those agencies decreased by 21 percent.[29]

The Reagan administration did not rely so heavily on reorganization strategies as earlier presidencies had. Although Reagan had promised during the campaign to abolish the Departments of Energy and Education (both had been created by the Carter administration), once elected the president chose to focus on budget cuts rather than complete elimination or reorganization of agencies. There were significant budget cuts and reductions in force across government, but, again, some agencies were targeted. By the middle of the second Reagan term, for example, the Department of Housing and Urban Development had seen its budget decrease by over 60 percent.[30]

In many agencies, there were lower-level internal reorganizations that were designed to facilitate political management. All of this was accompanied by the strident antibureaucratic rhetoric that had come to be known as "bureaucrat bashing." It should be noted that in some agencies, such as the Environmental Protection Agency, the Department of Housing and Urban Development, and the Department of the Interior, the legality of some of the actions taken by political executives was questioned and challenged; some appointees were found to have committed illegal acts.[31]

The Consolidating Presidency

After eight years of intensive political management during the Reagan presidency, the Bush administration came to office with a rather unclear set of objectives. Pfiffner notes:

> George Bush began his presidency with the politics of consolidation. The policy directions of the Reagan Administration were reinforced, but not extended, and the major trends in the conduct of the presidency were moderated, but not reversed. The White House Staff was not as dominant as it had been in recent administrations, Cabinet secretaries had more leeway, and political appointments were not as tightly controlled by the Office of Presidential Personnel.[32]

President Bush had a much less clear policy agenda and less need for a tightly controlled political management machine, but he confronted another problem in relation to political executives. The continuing link of the pay of top-level members of the civil service and political executives to that of Congress, coupled with the president's failure to recommend pay increases based on the Quadrennial Commission reports, had resulted in a significant gap between public-sector and private-sector pay.[33] President Bush found it difficult to recruit political appointees who would accept the salary; despite being overwhelmed with résumés, he was not able to attract the people he or his staff wanted for many of the positions. Further, the selection process was slowed because Bush had not permitted the formal establishment of a personnel office until after the election.

In many agencies, President Bush did not return to the numbers of appointees that had been present at the end of the Reagan term. There were exceptions, however, and those exceptions reflected the policy priorities of the Bush presidency. The Department of Justice and the State Department saw increased numbers of political Senior Executive Service appointments; Schedule C appointments remained at about the Reagan levels in the Departments of Agriculture, Education, Justice, and the Interior. President Bush appointed significantly higher numbers of Schedule Cs in the Departments of Energy, Commerce, and Labor, and the Environmental Protection Agency. At the direction of the White House, many of those Schedule Cs had to be in place before the secretaries were permitted to name lower-level appointees of their choice.[34]

At the same time, Bush veered sharply from his predecessor in consciously reaching out to the higher civil service in particular and the civil service in general. In 1989, on the tenth anniversary of the SES, he said, "As a public official, I have witnessed firsthand the positive influence of the SES system and have developed a deep respect for the men and women who make it work. Today, I rely on these executives to help translate our nation's goals and ideas into successful federal programs. They bring great expertise—and honor—to the field of public service."[35]

According to most observers, this rhetoric and a generally less aggressive presidential stance "took the edge off" the Bush administration's efforts to direct and control the higher civil service and the permanent bureaucracy. Nonetheless, the reliance on additional appointees to create, or maintain, an essentially hierarchical directing structure remained in place. Further, although President Bush did not increase the numbers of political appointees in some agencies, the total number of Schedule C appointments at the end of his term was still nearly double the nine hundred such appointments in place at the end of the Ford administration before the buildup began.[36]

The Clinton Presidency: Tentative Cooperation?

The Clinton administration came to Washington promising to "reinvent government" so that it could once again be a problem solver and not a problem. Clinton and his top staff also promised that those appointed to public office would more nearly reflect the rich diversity of the American population than had previous sets of appointees. The intense but chaotic White House screening activities that emerged from these promises produced an extremely slow appointment process. At midterm, however, there were clear signals that a strong reliance on political appointees would continue. The combined emphases on "reinventing government," performance review, and a revitalized bureaucracy necessitated a significant emphasis on political direction, so that the president's and the vice president's directives could be consistently reinforced. The president also began a new practice: the creation of performance contracts, which specified an agreement between the White House and the top political appointee in the department—the secretary—about program and policy objectives and measures. In some agencies this worked; in others, it did not.

Although the Clinton presidency was generally slow in the political appointment process, some agencies such as the Commerce Department were filled up with political appointments early. Eighteen months into the Clinton term, about sixteen hundred Schedule C appointments and seven hundred SES noncareer appointments had been made. Two hundred thirty-one of them were at Commerce.[37] Where the appointees were placed and how they were used in that case is not clear.

It is also notable that in the Clinton administration's major reinvention report, *Creating a Government that Works Better and Costs Less*,[38] there was no mention of any need for the political appointment process to be reinvented. Although a significant cut in the total number of career civil servants was recommended, no concomitant reduction in the number of political appointees was suggested. The use of larger numbers of political appointees, even when their purpose is not clear, appears to be a component of the Clinton management strategy, as it was of the strategies of those presidents who preceded him.

Questioning the Assumptions

Presidential management strategies, in various iterations and levels of intensity, are now an integral part of the contemporary merit system. Political management, reorganization, and "reinvention" all have other stated purposes—improved productivity, flexibility, responsiveness—but all are intended to change the way the merit system works. The paradox is that, while the system is clearly perceived to be a problem, these solutions generally do not address either its historic foundation or its legal complexity and constraints. The merit system has remained a square peg that does not fit into the round holes presidents propose.

There are other difficulties with reshaping merit through presidential direction, however. They include the ability of the White House to recruit qualified appointees, the willingness of those appointees to remain in office long enough to make a difference, and the realities of the managerial and policy relationships between political executives and members of the higher civil service. The role of Congress in light of expanded presidential authority is a separate, but fundamental, issue.

Do Presidents Have the Ability to Recruit the People They Need?

An obvious companion to the increased number of political appointees so central to presidential strategies is the ability to recruit the right people and to put them in the right places. This is an enormous problem that is rarely given adequate consideration. Presidents make about three thousand appointments; of these, slightly more than five hundred are at the top presidential appointment/Senate confirmation (PAS) level. About seventeen hundred are Schedule Cs, and the remainder (between seven hundred and eight hundred) are political appointments to the Senior Executive Service.[39] The presidential staff must concentrate on the highest appointments, those of people who are central to political and policy change. The selection of secretaries, under secretaries, and assistant secretaries consumes much of the transition period. At these high levels, policy expertise and management experience are important qualifications and are generally given careful consideration.

Key parts of the management strategies rely, however, on the lowest-level appointees, the Schedule Cs and first-level political members of the SES. If persons who do not possess the requisite management and policy skills to direct change successfully are placed in these lower positions, critical components of the strategies' assumptions are jeopardized. The ratio of appointees to career members of the higher civil service is about one to five, and it is the lower-level appointees who are in most frequent contact with the career civil service. Particularly in strategies such as those of the Reagan administration, in which career employees were consciously bypassed or isolated, lower-level appointees must have excellent management skills because they become the shadow managers. In practice, however, lower-level political appointments are most often made on the basis of campaign contributions or activity, rather than familiarity with either management or policy.[40]

Will the Appointees Stay?

An additional issue is the commitment of the appointees to staying in one position for a period that is long enough to permit them to effect change. As the Gaertners' study demonstrates, organizational and policy changes are long-term, disruptive, and often traumatic for many involved. Demanding change is rarely a successful strategy; consistent commitment and effort on the part of the leaders are important. Again, the expanded appointment system poses problems. Heclo termed the political executives he studied "strangers" from one another and from the career civil service.[41] More than a decade later, the National Commission on the Public Service noted that

> the average tenure of Presidential appointees during the Johnson Administration was 2.8 years; during the Nixon Administration it was 2.6 years; during the Carter Administration it was 2.5 years; and it was 2.0 years up to 1984 in the Reagan Administration. . . . From 1979 to 1986, non-career members of the Senior Executive Service remained in office an average of 20 months. Fully 40 percent of political executives throughout the government stayed in their positions less than one year.[42]

The tenure for Schedule Cs in one position was shorter than for any of the other appointees, with many remaining in one position for less than a year.

This tenure pattern not only causes problems for successful presidential direction of policy change; it renders virtually impossible any opportunity for the president to build constructive relationships with members of the career service. Surveys of former political appointees have demonstrated that, despite initial distrust, most appointees come to respect both the competence and the management expertise of senior career managers.[43] That process takes time, however, and respect for the career service cannot develop when appointees move frequently from position to position and from staff to staff. Further, the policy changes undertaken are likely to be limited and short-term so the political "short-timers" can see results before they leave. Fesler and Kettl summarize: "An administration loses sustained themes when burdened by a stop-and-go or go-and-stop process."[44]

Finally, consistent turnover causes the political recruiting and screening process to be nearly constant and time consuming for the presidential staff. If 40 percent of the appointees move every year, over a thousand new appointments must be made. The constant recruitment and appointment of new political members of the bureaucracy detracts from presidential policy initiatives, as well as from reasonable management practices.

Can Political Appointees Build a Management Team?

I have already noted the tension that exists between democratic change—the electoral cycle—and change in large bureaucratic organizations. Even in organizations that are flexible and open, leaders must have the ability to communicate a vision for change and development, and must create an organizational atmosphere in which change can be supported.[45] Because change itself is traumatic, the organizational climate must be one that fosters trust, communication, and teamwork. Public programs and organizations are complex and sometimes esoteric, so program and policy expertise must be added to the list of necessities.

The short tenure of many political appointees suggests strongly that, absent a partnership with senior career managers, political executives are unlikely to create a climate in which the changes they desire can be achieved. The creation of that partnership is initially jeopardized by the distrust with which many political executives approach their assignments and by the "wait-them-out" stance that can be adopted by career managers. The differences in perspectives on the organization itself and its policy priorities, on the quality of—and need for—the programs being administered, and on the quality of the career civil service staff in the organization exacerbate early problems.

Yet surveys and other data consistently demonstrate that, over time, political executives come to respect the competence and responsiveness of the career executives with whom they work and that career executives are willing to work with political appointees for change and redirection. Paul Light's analysis, done for the National Academy of Public Administration, demonstrates clearly that political executives who consider themselves prepared for the jobs they assume are the most likely to form constructive partnerships early on; it also found, however, that only half of the appointees studied considered themselves so prepared.[46] My case studies of three federal agencies found successful political/career management teams at the center of the successful policy changes I analyzed.[47] A recent analysis of the Senior Executive Service reported that, at the upper levels of the organization, it is increasingly difficult to draw fine lines between "political" responsibility and "career" responsibility: two-thirds of the career members surveyed reported speaking on behalf of programs or policies of their agencies; nearly half had testified before Congress; and nearly one-third had drafted legislation and worked for its passage. Nineteen percent had acted for a political appointee or served in a political position for an extended period.[48]

In this context, not sharing responsibilities is likely to be more difficult than sharing them. Further, the expertise that senior career managers offer in terms of managing within the confines of the civil service system is necessary if appointees are to "keep out of the bear-traps," as one former appointee put it. Another remembered that "[career] experience was absolutely invaluable. I needed them; it was essential. The career people kept me from shooting myself in the foot."[49] While this is not to suggest that all career managers are angels and political executives are dolts for not recognizing this, it does underline the extent to which simplistic assumptions about hierarchical management in the public sector and about managing in a civil service system can be misleading. As James Pfiffner accurately observes:

> Resistance to presidential directives is inevitable, but it is important to keep in mind that this resistance stems from members of Congress, interest groups, and the leadership of executive branch agencies. . . . Using the career service as a scapegoat for all resistance to presidential desires may be comforting, but it does not represent an accurate analysis of power in Washington.[50]

Further, it must be noted that, no matter how overwhelming a president or his appointees perceive an electoral mandate to be, legal and ethical behavior remains a hallmark of the public service. That sense of duty and responsibility has been well instilled in the highest levels of the career service; adherence to its principles should not be viewed as an obstacle to presidential direction or as a lack of responsiveness. As experiences in both the Nixon and Reagan administrations demonstrated, losing sight of that common ground is costly. Common commitment to it should be a key component of presidential management strategies; it can then serve as the basis for a constructive political/career partnership.

Where Is Congress?

The first chapters of this book described the debates about the direction of the public service and the concern that a centralized civil service would abrogate constitutional provisions for shared responsibility for the executive branch. Where, in all the extensive presidential direction and control efforts just described, is Congress? Has that institution also tried to increase its influence over the civil service? How do congressional efforts fit with, or contradict, presidential efforts? And where does all of this leave the civil service and merit? Newland offers a firm assessment:

> Aggrandizement of presidential power is increasingly an irresistible force in American politics and government; . . . and presidents use their ever growing political power to advance partisan self-interests in civil service reform as in other matters. . . . The politics of special interests greatly control both Congress and the presidency in civil service legislation. . . . those special interests support major legislative changes . . . so long as their particular interests are also advanced or at least insulated.[51]

Certainly the move toward giving more power to the president had been evident since the Brownlow committee report, even though there was sporadic congressional resistance. The general congressional reaction to presidential reform initiatives has been to reject those that are seen as clearly granting too much power to the president, but to approve reforms that "seem to be entirely abstract, . . . or to involve only the harmless matters of process that are the passion of professors of public administration."[52] The "matters of process," however, cannot be lightly dismissed. They are the core of the civil service system and the reason for most of the external efforts to control it.

Congress has had a reactive strategy of its own, which has imposed additional hierarchical controls on bureaucratic organizations and managers. Although these actions have been less coherent and predictable than the presidential management initiatives, they have echoed the same "fraud, waste, and abuse" theme. They have also had the effect of dramatically increasing the complexity of the public management environment. The congressional actions fall into two general categories: increased use of formal accountability mechanisms, such as inspectors general; and greatly increased micromanagement, which involves building administrative processes and mechanisms into legislation.[53]

Inspectors General and the Civil Service

The combination of the inspectors-general controls with civil service reform is a classic outcome of the debate that Light refers to as "the confusion about whether to free the civil service or imprison it."[54] Although the initial legislation covered only eleven executive departments, with the intent of creating new internal surveillance offices to report wrongdoing to Congress, ten years later most federal departments and agencies were covered. As with many other reforms, the inspectors-general legislation had purportedly technical objectives: to promote "economy, efficiency and effectiveness" and to "prevent and detect fraud and abuse."[55] Inspectors general report to both the president and Congress. Their information is valuable to both, but for Congress the reports clearly provide new access to internal bureaucratic and executive-branch (including political-appointee) data. Even during times of significant budget cuts and staff reductions across government, the staff of the Office of Inspectors General grew substantially, to a total of about twelve thousand by 1992.

In his excellent analysis of the impact of the inspectors-general controls, Light observes that their efforts attack waste after it has occurred, and do little to correct problems at the source. Those problems, he argues, are too many layers of controls and directives, outdated budget and financial systems, and the failure to create incentives "for doing the right thing in the first place."[56]

Micromanaging the Bureaucracy

The staff of the Congress has expanded dramatically in the past twenty years. In 1990, the Congress had nearly thirty-one thousand employees; that is three times the 1970 level.[57] That number includes members of personal staffs, of the many congressional committees and subcommittees, and of congressional agencies such as the General Accounting Office and the Congressional Budget Office. Both the increased number and the increased opportunity for contact with executive-branch employees through committee and subcommittee oversight are important.

As is the case with the authority of the president to direct the executive branch, the authority of the Congress to maintain and use oversight mechanisms is not in question. Rather, it is the nature, quality, and impact of those mechanisms that is relevant to the merit system. The question, Kettl argues, is not "whether Members of Congress should oversee, often in microscopic detail, administrators and their programs, for it is inevitable that they will do so . . . [but what] effects micromanagement has on the policy process."[58] For my purposes here, the question extends to micromanagement's effects on those who administer public policies and manage public programs.

Burdette Loomis and others have described a pattern in Congress that is similar to that described for transient political employees. Members of Congress and their staffers take on short-term, accessible goals to the detriment of issues and actions that are longer-term, more difficult, and more important.[59] This legislative pattern produces the same results as political appointees' demands for fast action. The legislative demands, however, target different activities and add congressional monitoring controls to the internal bureaucratic maze. Kettl summarizes the impact: "In such a system, everyone is reactive: Members of Congress who react to problems that emerge; top agency officials who fear programmatic or budgetary retribution; and lower-level administrators who avoid rocking the boat. The result, of course, is that nothing happens quickly or well."[60]

In the pulling and hauling between the president and the Congress, then, the permanent bureaucracy remains a target for control. The pattern of involvement is similar in both cases: discretion for members of the career service is to be limited whenever possible; control is to be exerted through additional levels of political appointees or other staff members responsible to the president or Congress; and accountability will be defined as responsiveness to that control.

So What?

The civil service system is complicated and often contradictory; efforts to reform that system have most often increased its complexity and unwieldiness. Presidential and congressional efforts to direct and control only add to the potluck quality of merit. In addition, they have had the somewhat perverse effect of creating outcomes that are different from those intended.

Efforts to constrain bureaucratic discretion by adding more layers of controls, for example, actually create more discretion. In a system with so many masters and conflicting directions, it is impossible for someone to follow or be responsive to them all. The career civil servant must choose which to follow and which to ignore. The more choices, the more discretion. At the same time, the many layers of controls stifle good management. Because micromanagement, whether by Congress or by the president, is narrow and temporary, it precludes the use of broader strategies and the consideration of long-term solutions. It forces managers and executives into a reactive stance and causes an already rule-bound system to become even more tentative and conservative in its actions. Further, because accountability is so clearly defined by external overhead mechanisms, rule-following behavior, rather than effective management, is rewarded.

Management, in fact, suffers because responsibility for it has become so diffuse and because those who have assumed ever-increasing managerial responsibilities—the president and the Congress—are those with the least experience and expertise in managing. The management expertise that exists in the higher civil service is seen as a force to be limited and controlled, rather than as a resource to be used. It is not surprising that the system still does not work. It is critical, however, that the merit system and the public service be effective. The changing nature of public work, the changing functions of government, and the changing nature of the workforce argue for a thorough reassessment of what merit is about and how it fits with both responsiveness to direction and the real need for excellent public management. How these issues are being redefined can be clarified by an examination of how government, government work, and government workers are changing, and what future demands are likely to be.

Chapter Seven

Changing Work,

Changing Workforce,

Changing Expectations

The federal merit system owes much of its jerry-built quality and incremental growth to politics and political values. However, public personnel systems have been influenced by other forces as well. Major economic developments and events that shaped government activities also shaped the government's workforce and the nature of its work. The policy of veterans' preference profoundly influenced the demographic composition of public bureaucracies, as did social injustices such as racial, gender, and age discrimination.

The system responded to some changes, but remained remarkably impervious to others. Government recruiting practices, based since 1883 on the principle of opening the system to all but then screening by neutral competitive examination, remained in place even after there was solid evidence that they were discriminatory and did not fit with the realities of the contemporary workforce.[1] Similarly, a rigidly standardized classification system remains in place despite clear evidence that it does not meet rapidly changing organizational needs and that it does, in fact, contribute to a serious lack of diversity at the middle and upper levels of many public organizations.[2]

Although the structures and systems remained stable, the ground under them shifted in the 1980s. The nature of government work was redefined significantly by the practices of privatization and contracting out. Government employees who had been program and policy experts and deliverers of government services increasingly were called upon to be contract managers. At the same time, as budgets and permanent agency staffs were cut, the missions of the agencies remained the same or were expanded. This caused civil servants to be not only contract managers, but large-scale contract managers, as more agency responsibilities were contracted out.

Some organizations were pushed to their analytical and policy limits by unprecedented tasks and challenges; for example, environmental agencies struggled with ways to clean up severely damaging pollution, while the U.S. Department of Energy explored ways to dispose of radioactive waste in a way that would be safe for hundreds of years and generations of new citizens. The need for the government to be "smart," to use Donald Kettl's term, became immediate and profound.[3]

The changing nature of government work was accompanied in many organizations, both private and public, by the reality of a changing workforce. The demographics of that workforce are important. There are more two-career families in the workforce than ever before in history. The labor pool from which the workforce is drawn is changing; the extent to which the skills of those in the labor pool will meet emerging demands is not clear. Further, a substantial portion of the population is aging. Many already in the workforce will face dual personal responsibilities: two-career families will be responsible for day care and other services for their children, but will also be confronted with the need to care for aging parents and relatives. The members of this "sandwich generation" will require flexibility and support if they are to remain effective and productive workers.

All these developments have occurred in an environment of changing expectations for government and widespread dissatisfaction with its performance. Vice President Gore's National Performance Review announced that its intent was to fix a government that was "not simply broke; it is broken."[4] The report explicitly recognized the underlying problem on its first page: "The National Performance Review . . . is also about closing the *trust* deficit: proving to the American people that their tax dollars will be treated with respect for the hard work that earned them."[5]

The combined effect of these influences on public organizations and on the systems that support their operation is significant. To achieve a better understanding of the nature of the challenges these factors pose for the merit system and for the fundamental principles that have informed it for more than one hundred years, it is useful to examine each of the influences in more detail.

The Changing Nature of Government Work

The civil service system was created to recruit, hire, and compensate employees for jobs that were assumed to be routine and amenable to standardization. Early employees delivered mail, built roads, and performed clerical and financial tasks. Common sense and basic skills were considered adequate preparation for most civil service jobs. Formal education entered the picture later, as did the increasing professionalization of the career civil service and the concomitant influences of professional norms and values.[6]

Rather quickly, however, both the nature and the scope of government work began to change. As early as 1935, the Commission on Inquiry of Public Service Personnel noted that

> in frontier days, . . . government was plain and society simple. The frontiersman was a jack-of-all-trades, and a jack-of-all-trades was quite competent to perform any of the duties imposed by public office. . . . [However,] as a result of changes in society and government it became necessary to formulate new methods of personnel control, based on the new division of work. The jack-of-all-trades had to make way for the expert.[7]

The force of change became more intense with the advent of the New Deal and the public policies and programs it created. The programs developed during that time added new levels of complexity to the services delivered by government. Many of the new public-works programs demanded engineering and scientific expertise; social-welfare programs demanded knowledge of human behavior and motivation; the growth of government demanded greater knowledge of organizations and management.

The need for a well-educated public workforce grew exponentially in the years following World War II. Charles Levine and Rosslyn Kleeman note that in the years from 1960 to 1980, "the number of engineers on the federal civilian payroll increased by more than 50 percent, to about 100,000. The number of computer specialists increased by more than 600 percent, to around 34,000."[8]

As the nature of government work changed, so, too, did government organizations and the internal employee mix. Again, Levine and Kleeman provide an apt summary:

> The large-scale, pyramid-shaped organization with executives at the top, line supervisors in the middle, and armies of clerks at the bottom is giving way to more complicated arrangements of authority and communication. New organ-

izations often have an "egg-shaped" form because they employ a larger number of middle-level professionals than clerks. . . . [This,] in part, reflects the growth in the number of professional and technical employees resulting from changing technology, legislated program changes (for example, the creation of new agencies such as the Environmental Protection Agency), and the necessity of employing large numbers of middle-level managers to coordinate contracts with organizations outside the federal government.[9]

This suggests two significant trends in government work. First, government organizations and employees are increasingly required to undertake technological and scientific tasks that require advanced knowledge and scientific ability. Organizations and employees must have the ability to learn and to use new information quickly and effectively. The reactive mode so often associated with bureaucrats and their organizations does not help in meeting the new demands.[10]

Second, an increasing amount of government work is being performed by people who are not government employees. The implications of this trend are numerous; two of the most significant are that government employees are increasingly contract managers rather than direct service providers, and that, to a significant but currently unknown extent, critical expertise and knowledge are neither generated nor retained within government.

Contracting Out and Managing Contractors

Contracting out—or, in Kettl's phrase, "government by proxy"—has a long history in the United States.[11] Federal procurement offices have always purchased a wide variety of goods and services. The federal government has for many years passed money to state and local governments for the actual delivery of services. Many categorical-grant programs arising from the War on Poverty and other efforts in the 1960s directed funds to not-for-profit organizations for service delivery. Federal spending on contracts for research and development increased from about $100 million annually just before World War II to more than $10 billion by the 1960s. Before the war, research-and-development activities financed by the federal government were generally conducted in and by government institutions. By the 1960s, 80 percent of those activities were conducted in nongovernmental institutions.[12] More recently, the call to privatize many government services, or at least to move their delivery from government organizations to the private sector, has influenced the amount of contracting out. H. Brinton Milward notes that the total dollar amount spent for the contracting out of services nearly doubled in the period from 1980 to 1990, increasing from $47.6 billion in 1980 to $90.6 billion ten years later. Most of the increase occurred before 1986, in the first Reagan term.[13]

Contractors perform many kinds of services for the government. In the Department of Defense, contractors build major weapons systems, provide training and education programs, and design computer systems, as well as performing numerous other tasks. In other agencies, as the total number of full-time employees declined, the role of contractors expanded. Milward cites Kettl on the case of the Environmental Protection Agency and its Superfund program, which was intended to clean up the country's most severely polluted sites:

> Contractors researched Freedom of Information Act requests received by the agency. They drafted memos for top EPA officials. They prepared congressional testimony. They wrote regulations and drafted international agreements on behalf of EPA. They trained and wrote statements of work for other contractors and then evaluated their performance. They even wrote the Superfund program's annual report to Congress.[14]

The EPA is not alone in this regard. The Department of Energy has many more contract than full-time employees; the National Aeronautics and Space Administration relies heavily on contractors to provide basic research, as well as to do other tasks central to the effective performance of the agency's mission. The Department of Energy relies so heavily on contractors and has so many of them that it "bundles" contracts and hires other contractors to manage them. Both the National Performance Review and the General Accounting Office have explicitly criticized the Department of Energy for both the quality of its contracts and its ability to manage them.

The actual extent of the practice of contracting out and its impact on government work are difficult to determine. Data are very limited and often mask the real nature of work being carried out under contract. The gross dollar figures demonstrate an increasing reliance on contracting and contractors in many agencies, however, and there are clear implications for the civil service employees responsible for contract management. Clearly, new skills are required. The technical and professional skills needed by a successful engineer, for example, do not necessarily translate into the effective design or management of engineering contracts. In this sense, the recruiting, classification, and training activities of the federal government lag far behind—or worse, fail completely to match—the reality of what many employees do on a daily basis.

There are also critical issues of accountability. Again, Kettl succinctly summarizes:

> Government has relied on contractors not only to provide it with goods and services, but also to tell it what it ought to buy, to evaluate what it has purchased, and to manage many of the steps in between, including writing testimony for government officials to present to Congress explaining the transactions. If the government is not a smart buyer, the critical responsibility for the performance of public programs passes to its contractors. Government cannot be sovereign if it cannot buy smart.[15]

Finally, there are important issues related to what skills, knowledge, and expertise public employees and organizations *must* retain. Can government managers be smart managers, or the government a smart buyer, if critical knowledge and abilities are fostered outside the government but not matched by it? Obviously the government cannot and should not do everything. The questions of what it should do and what it must know, however, are central to the future of an effective public service and merit system. Those questions have not been directly asked or answered in the current trend toward increased contracting.

Contracting out and other reforms such as reinvention, reengineering, and total quality management have had other significant effects on government work and government organizations. One of the most important is the changed, and greatly diminished, role they have created for middle management. The flatter, more flexible organizations that these reforms envision and create do not need so many middle managers as did the old hierarchical structures. Nor will they use those that remain in the same way. How midlevel managers will function in these emerging organizations is not yet clear; the linking system that they provide, however, will remain central.

Contracting out and related practices are not, then, panaceas for the problems of government. Indeed, these activities can create unanticipated problems for public organizations and their employees. They have certainly created a climate inside government that demands new skills and sensibilities. This fresh view of what government actually does has not been reflected in debates about the future of the public service, nor have previous reforms addressed the issue. Unfortunately, the trend toward what Milward calls "hollow government"[16] is only one of several that must be considered if the full complexity of the future public service is effectively to be addressed. Changing demographics and changing expectations for government are also part of the puzzle.

Demographic Trends and Changes

As the nature of government work was changing, the nature of the national workforce and the labor pool that would feed that workforce were changing as well. Women entered the workforce in increasing numbers: between 1975 and 1990, the number of women in the labor force increased by 51 percent.[17] It is expected to increase still further in the next two decades, but at a slower rate. Entry into and participation in the labor force are also projected to increase for African Americans, Asians, and Hispanics, but the increase will be largest for Hispanic groups. Seventy-nine percent of the 1990 labor force consisted of non-Hispanic whites. By 2005, that figure is expected to decline to about 73 percent. In the same period, Hispanic representation will increase from 8 percent to slightly more than 11 percent.[18]

These changes will be represented in the federal workforce, perhaps disproportionately. As Levine noted, "For many women, minorities, and first-generation college graduates, the corporate world has been seen as an alien place, while the civil service, with its social and ethnic diversity, affirmative action programs, and merit based entrance and promotion systems, has been regarded as a socially comfortable place to pursue a career." [19] Indeed, Office of Personnel Management data indicate that employment in all affirmative-action categories except veterans has increased since 1988, with larger numbers of women moving into upper-level and middle management positions.[20]

Managing this new diversity effectively and taking full advantage of the opportunities it offers, however, will be difficult for many public organizations. Despite the many management education and training programs aimed at fostering better communication and participation among members of an organization and at recognizing the value that added diversity brings, significant tensions continue to be present in some organizations. Addressing these issues in a positive way will be a fundamental part of good management in the future.

Other demographic trends also have significance for the federal workforce. The aging of the population and the labor force is a leading example. Lower fertility rates combined with longer life expectancies and the aging of the baby-boom generation are having an important impact on the age composition of American society. There are both more elderly persons generally and more in the "special needs" elderly category—those over eighty who require special health care or supervisory attention. The growth of these elderly populations is important for several reasons. Clearly, the nature of the services required will change and the role of government in meeting these needs will change as well. At a time when more people will begin to draw on Social Security benefits, fewer people will be contributing funds. Some studies suggest that the ratio of support will decline from 5:1 in 1985 to 2.5:1 in the next thirty years.[21]

Quite aside from the significant policy and service-delivery implications, the aging of the population will change the workforce enormously. This is due in large part to the increase in the workforce of families in which both husbands and wives are employed. In 1960, only 31.6 percent of working husbands' wives were employed outside the home. By 1990, that figure was nearly 70 percent.[22] Further, many of these two-career families have young children. Again, the figure has increased dramatically: in 1960, only 18.6 percent of married women with a spouse present and children under the age of six were in the civilian labor force. By 1990, nearly 60 percent of such women were employed outside the home. The percentage of women with children in the next age category—six to seventeen—nearly doubled from 1960 to 1990.[23]

What this means for employers is quite simple. These workers not only will be responsible for the care of their young children but, in many cases, will assume responsibility for their elderly parents and other relatives as well. They will do this while continuing to juggle the responsibilities and tensions of full-time jobs. Improved day care, elder care, flextime, and flexibility about the place one works will assume more central roles in efforts to recruit and retain qualified and productive workers. Many agencies that have traditionally relied on a mobile workforce, or that have required mobility as a condition of promotion, will be confronted with a workforce that cannot and will not move.

Another substantial portion of the federal workforce will be aging as the baby-boom generation matures. Because the federal workforce is older than the national workforce in general, this trend assumes special significance.[24] Issues of retaining and motivating these workers as the nature of government work changes—and, in many cases, becomes more complex and technical—must also be considered. Retraining, continuing education, pension and other retirement-benefit reforms, and classification reforms that permit flexible use of the existing workforce will become crucial parts of human-resource-management strategies. The *Civil Service 2000* report observed that

federal agencies can either "buy" or "make" the skills they need. . . . they can recruit and hire highly skilled, qualified workers from the national labor market, or they can invest in their current workers and teach them what they need to know. Since many federal employers will continue to face difficulties in competing for the best qualified workers, federal agencies should systematically invest more in their existing workforces.[25]

The demographic issues faced by the federal government will be confronted by the private sector and by most state and local governments as well. At present, however, little is being done to meet the new challenges and take advantage of the new opportunities. In terms of the aging workforce, for example, the General Accounting Office reported that "as with most private sector organizations . . . the federal government does not have an overall strategy to address the challenges arising from workforce aging."[26] The GAO report emphasized the need to develop such a strategy, however: "The first members of the baby boom generation will reach age 55 in the year 2001, with the last of them reaching age 55 by 2019. Because the baby boom generation is huge—76 million—and the following generation is considerably smaller, a greater proportion of the workforce will be eligible to retire . . . between 2001 and 2019 than at any point in American history."[27]

Overall, the changing demographics of the labor pool and the federal workforce point clearly to the need to reconsider carefully the fundamental elements of civil service systems and governmental strategies for human-resource management. The long-established practice of screening large numbers of applicants and potential employees has already been challenged; many organizations with specialized technical and educational needs have developed targeted recruiting strategies aimed at luring the limited number of qualified persons to government. The same is true of the search for greater diversity in federal agencies. Specialized recruiting strategies, designed at the agency and even the program level, have replaced the standard centralized recruiting and examining procedures. Agencies such as those in the Department of Defense have argued that existing systems cannot respond to changing demographics and different workforce skills and needs; these agencies have already asked Congress to consider systems for human-resource management and compensation separate from those of the broader system. The extent to which the federal civil service can change to meet these new challenges will be an important determinant of the extent to which it will be able to serve its role in government and governance. Further, neutral competence and efficiency based on standardization—so prized by reformers through the years—have become, and will continue to be, more difficult to define and more difficult to recognize in practice.

Changing work and a changing workforce are not the only issues of change facing governments and civil service systems, however. There are new demands for increased productivity, for greater flexibility and innovation, and for improved responsiveness to elected officials and citizens—the newly defined "customers" of the public service. Expectations for government performance rose again in the 1990s, but were accompanied by a demanding new agenda for change.

Changing Expectations

The history of the federal merit system has been characterized by a series of efforts to reform its operations, efforts that reflected the profound ambivalence that marks American attitudes about public bureaucracy. On the one hand, there is a desire to see the public service be more open, more flexible, and more adaptive. On the other, there is a deep-seated distrust of bureaucratic power and a desire to control it. In the 1970s and 1980s, the balance tipped clearly toward control.

The Clinton election signaled a renewed sense that government organizations and their employees could be problem solvers and could participate as partners in the important processes of governing. There was a caveat, however: government had to be reinvented first. The challenges posed by the reinvention initiatives were enormous, both for those who would design the changes and for those who would implement them. The opportunity to "break out of the boxes" was perhaps unparalleled, but the hazards of doing so were also obvious. Most notably for the career civil servants who would be central to the success or failure of reinvention, great risks and considerable uncertainty accompanied the proposed changes. The tensions inherent in the opportunity for real change, the uncertainty of the path toward it, and the risks, both personal and organizational, that such change would engender, created yet another complex dimension to the proposed activities.

As these politically directed changes were being designed,[28] there were also other reforms inside federal agencies that were having an impact on employees and their expectations about the nature of their work. As was the case with previous management reforms, the most recent were drawn from the private sector. Total-quality-management initiatives and programs, emphasizing employee participation and empowerment and customer satisfaction, were instituted in most agencies. Employee teams became key problem-solving units and decision makers.

A more limited number of organizations undertook more dramatic reforms, attempting to reconfigure their organizational structures to reflect key processes and systems rather than traditional functions. This reengineering mandated fundamental internal changes in leadership, management, and structure. Although some of the early efforts at reengineering, such as those at the Internal Revenue Service and the Department of Defense, operated within the confines of the existing civil service system, the challenges they pose to that system are the most compelling in its history.[29] In combination with reinvention initiatives, reengineering changes attack the very foundation of the existing system.

The Changing Face of Reform

For nearly one hundred years, reforms have been added to the base created by the Pendleton Act in 1883. In many respects, Jimmy Carter's "comprehensive" reform did the same. Civil service processes and activities continued to operate in the realms of standardized testing, classification, and compensation. The changing nature of government work, a heightened dissatisfaction with the ability of government to change and act more flexibly, and particularly the emphases in total quality management on customer service and the satisfaction of those outside the organization challenged the constraints of these activities.

The alluring simplicity of the principles of reinventing government also challenged the complexity and the murkiness of the existing system. The election of President Clinton and his creation of the National Performance Review (NPR) under the direction of Vice President Gore provided the opportunity for some of the principles to become part of government reform efforts. As originally outlined by David Osborne and Ted Gaebler and translated through the NPR, the principles include: [30]

1. Cutting red tape
2. Putting customers first
3. Empowering employees to get results
4. Cutting back to basics: producing better government for less

Some of these principles or objectives are reminiscent of past reforms; the idea of cutting red tape is certainly not new, nor is that of reducing the cost of government. Empowering employees, on the other hand, directly confronts fundamental tenets of earlier reforms. It certainly conflicts with the hierarchical authority and management strategy of traditional bureaucratic organizations and the civil service system. Yet the National Performance Review made a commitment to all of them: "They fit together much like the pieces of a puzzle: if one is missing, the others lose their power. To create organizations that deliver value to American taxpayers, we must embrace all four." [31]

Other elements of the philosophy of reinvention also attack the existing orthodoxy. Osborne and Gaebler and the National Performance Review advocate that government employees "steer more and row less." This makes good sense in terms of efficiency and effectiveness; it confronts head on the traditional conundrum of the proper policy role for career civil servants and raises accountability issues as well. The nostrum provided by Woodrow Wilson and again by the first director of the Bureau of the Budget in 1923 is firmly embedded in American administrative thought: "We in the Bureau of the Budget are not concerned with matters of policy. . . . The President and Congress determine which way the ship sails, for that is a matter of policy, but we in the hold of the ship have something to do with how far she can sail through the way in which, in our humbler place, we apply common sense business principles."[32]

The extent to which "steering" is—or is perceived to be—equated with policymaking is important to the outcome of the "reinventing government" initiative. Even though it is clear that members of the civil service do, in fact, participate in policy decisions, often in significant ways, the legitimacy of that activity is one of the sticking points of reform.

Kettl addresses the accountability issue related to the "steering/rowing" debate. "If government is to steer," he notes, "someone will have to keep the compass."[33] The point that, as central and hierarchical controls are discarded, some central guidance and monitoring remains necessary is well taken. In reforms around the world, but most notably in New Zealand, Australia, and the United Kingdom, greater flexibility and discretion have translated into extensive decentralization with little or no "center." The National Performance Review and the reinvention initiative fell into the same pattern: activities were to be carried out primarily at the agency level, with no central interference or monitoring. But, in a government obsessed with accountability, where does it reside in such a system?

The Reinvention Process

The National Performance Review, like the Civil Service Reform Act before it, relied heavily on the expertise of career civil servants to analyze the various ways in which government was "broke and broken." The analysis of the problems and preparation of the report operated on a tight time schedule; President Clinton announced the formation of the NPR in March 1993 and the report was presented to him in September 1993. It contained 384 major recommendations. They addressed problems in twenty-seven agencies, but also recommended changes in major systems such as personnel, information management, procurement, and budgeting.

The report explicitly acknowledged its reliance on concepts such as total quality management and business process reengineering, but also noted that

> these management disciplines were developed for the private sector, where conditions are quite different. . . . private sector doctrines tend to overlook some central problems of government: its monopolies, its lack of a bottom line, its obsession with process, rather than results. . . . In a large corporation, transformation takes 6 to 8 years at best. In the federal government, which has 7 times as many employees as America's largest corporation, it will undoubtedly take longer to bring about the historic changes we propose.[34]

The recommendations clarify the dramatic scope of the changes the NPR proposed. One set of them, for example, advocated the complete abolition of the Federal Personnel Manual and large reductions in the total numbers of "oversight" employees: those in personnel, financial management, and budget. Another recommended that the Department of Agriculture close or consolidate twelve hundred field offices and that the Departments of Housing and Urban Development, Education, Energy, and Commerce, among others, significantly cut back offices and operations. A complete redefinition of the labor/management relationship in government—from combative to collaborative—was proposed, and the National Partnership Council was created. The report even included a dozen recommendations aimed at improving the operation and efficiency of the executive office of the president.

As noted above, the National Performance Review process emphasized activities within each agency. Reinvention teams and "reinvention laboratories" were created to focus on agency-specific reforms. In most cases, these activities were directed by senior staffers from the Office of the Secretary, a move intended to demonstrate the commitment of the top departmental leaders to reinvention. Because these activities would be carried out in each department and agency and in full view of many agency employees, it was hoped that employee commitment to the overall changes would be strengthened.

The expectation that federal employees and the systems that support—or constrain—them could and would change as the NPR envisioned is inherent in the recommendations. The expectation that unfettered employees would be creative and flexible problem solvers is also consistently present. The difficulty in moving from the expectation to the reality was highlighted by the General Accounting Office in an early assessment of the NPR and its recommendations:

> Underlying many of the NPR report's recommendations is the assumption that agencies have the processes, systems and qualified staff in place to accept the increased authority and responsibility that come with the deregulation and decentralization contemplated by the NPR. However, our management reviews of 23 large federal agencies and departments done over the last decade consistently have shown that many agencies lack the fundamental underpinnings that will be needed.[35]

The General Accounting Office also noted the need for a congressional/presidential partnership if many of the recommendations were to be enacted and implemented. Congressional efforts, such as the passage of the Government Performance and Results Act of 1993, demonstrate the juncture of the interests of the president and Congress in that regard. On the other hand, congressional actions on some reinvention initiatives such as downsizing federal agencies, streamlining service delivery, and simplifying overhead controls reveal the continued presence of congressional self-interest.

The success of the Clinton/Gore reinvention effort is also related to the long-term leadership necessary for effective change. The NPR report did not address the issue of political appointees and executives, but it became apparent early in the Clinton term that the emphasis on larger numbers of political appointments would continue. The extent to which those appointees overcome the patterns of earlier administrations and form effective working partnerships with the career executives who will actually manage the change will be another important factor in the success or failure of reinvention.

What all this suggests is that the opportunities presented by the most recent reform proposals are confounded by many of the same issues that tangled earlier efforts. The National Performance Review and its proposals to reinvent government correctly identified many of the problems of the contemporary civil service. The support of the president and the active leadership of the vice president gave the reinvention initiative a level of visibility and credibility not often found in reform efforts. The conviction held by many career executives and managers that change was necessary and possible provided fertile ground for reforms in many agencies and departments; the existence of the more open structures and decision-making processes created by total quality efforts reinforced the potential. Why would there be problems?

There would be problems because the changes required the full participation of partnerships that have historically been difficult to create and maintain: congressional/presidential, political/career, and labor/management. The emphasis on customer service and satisfaction clearly implied a new and more equal partnership between civil servant and citizen as well. The inherently political nature of these partnerships was an important variable in the reform equation.

In addition, the nature of the public service and the role of the career civil servant were essentially redefined by reinvention objectives. The elimination of rules, regulations, and other procedural restraints and controls creates a system in which individual discretion is prized and rewarded and accountability is profoundly different. The legitimate boundaries of discretion and flexibility became an issue; the freedom to fail as well to succeed in the exercise of that discretion also needs to be considered.

Finally, the effort to reinvent, rather than to tinker at the fringes of, existing systems raised a new kind of question: What was important to keep? Was there anything in the merit system and in the principles and procedures that it spawned that remained fundamental to good government and governance? What was it? How did it fit with the objectives of the new reforms? In the pursuit of flexibility and decentralization, for example, did any government-wide objectives and standards persist? What were they? What, if any, was the role of a central agency for human-resource management such as the Office of Personnel Management?

That organization has never fulfilled its potential; from its initially promising start, it quickly became a political arm of the White House during the Reagan presidency. Efforts to rebuild it during the Bush administration were notable, but its decline during the Clinton presidency was precipitous. The OPM should have been a leader in reform efforts and activities. Instead, it was nearly invisible.

The need for a central agency that articulates and clarifies government-wide objectives and standards, that provides long-term, strategic advice about changes and issues relevant to human-resource management, that monitors successful management and change strategies in federal organizations, and that provides advice and support to those agencies that do not have well-developed management capacities has never been greater. The Clinton administration's reforms at the Office of Management and Budget, the traditional "challenger" in this regard, emphasize this need. As was outlined in "OMB 2000," Leon Panetta, the director of the agency, reorganized it to integrate more effectively its several roles, including budget analysis, management review, and policy development. In the process, the management side of the OMB was eliminated. Management activities were integrated with budget reviews in newly created offices of resource management. Many have argued that management never had priority at the OMB; at the time Jimmy Carter's Civil Service Reform Act was passed, for example, Scotty Campbell announced that it was his intent to "take the 'M' from OMB," where, he said, it had never been used.[36]

Nonetheless, the significant reduction in both visibility and responsibility for management activities at the OMB, in combination with the general ineffectiveness of the Office of Personnel Management, has created a void in the federal government precisely when management is most needed. The "keeping of the compass" that Kettl and others see as a necessary component of effective reinvention becomes even more elusive in this setting.

Conclusion

As the federal civil service system moved through the early part of its second century, its very foundation was questioned and shaken. It did not appear likely that the system that had evolved in the twentieth century could meet the challenges of the twenty-first. Unfortunately, it was still not clear what the key components of a new system to replace the old would be, and many of the troublesome characteristics of earlier reform efforts remained in place. Problems of legitimacy and accountability of the civil service and its members remained acute. Political consensus about the dimensions of change and new authority and flexibility for public employees appeared tenuous; the potential for effective partnerships between the president and the Congress, between political executives and career managers, between labor and management, and between citizens and those who serve them remained troublesome. Even with agreement about the need for government to create and maintain a workforce that reflected the requisite skills and expertise and with new confidence in government's ability to be a problem solver, debate continued about the scope of the government in which those skills should be used. Significant downsizing became a central part of reinvention reform; issues of good management and managing change did not.

The issues identified in the introduction to this book as central to the civil service and to merit assumed even greater importance. As the system itself was questioned, the balances between politics and merit, between neutral competence and responsiveness, and between efficiency and effectiveness have been reconsidered and redefined. This has happened in the context of changing work and a changing workforce. The questions that have been raised, the potential answers, and the fit of both with the emerging realities of government organizations and organization are the topics of the final chapter.

Chapter Eight

Transforming

Merit

"The governments of the United States," James Wilson wrote, "were not designed to be efficient or powerful, but to be tolerable and malleable." [1] For much of its history, the federal civil service has not met the standards of efficiency imposed on it; it has become notoriously unmalleable, and for many citizens and elected officials it is barely tolerable. It has, however, become increasingly powerful. Whether or not there is now merit in the merit system, it is a major force in government and governance and is fundamental to the effectiveness of both.

Efforts at reform have generally not met their objectives. They have, in fact, often reinforced the problems they were intended to solve and have strengthened bureaucratic power, while simultaneously diminishing overall effectiveness. Michael Nelson labels this the "grand irony" of American bureaucracy: that "repeated efforts to bring government under political branch control have enhanced the power of bureaucracy." [2] The irony underlines the central theme of this book: the turbulent relationship between politics and merit has increasingly defined the merit system in fundamentally negative terms. The failure to define a positive role for the civil service has limited its capacity and prestige, but has paradoxically increased its discretion and power. The desired equilibrium has yet to be attained.

As a result, the modern civil service is having trouble meeting even its most basic objectives: recruiting qualified personnel, rewarding and motivating those employees, and organizing them to pursue and meet public goals. These are straightforward objectives. Why have even they become problematic? The answer has to do with both the political foundation of merit and the structures and procedures that have been built on it.

Rigid structures and stable procedures do not support many of the problem-solving activities in which public employees are now engaged. The overwhelming emphasis on inputs and processes, rather than outcomes, that characterizes many components of the civil service reinforces this problem. Michael Barzelay, in arguing that new systems must "break through bureaucracy," describes earlier reforms that transferred private techniques into public organizations as "trouble waiting to happen," because "one key concept—the product—did not make the journey from industry to government."[3] That concept and customer satisfaction are fundamental parts of the current round of reforms and of techniques such as total quality management; these reforms suggest a basic restructuring of the system.

In large part, too, the troubles with the current system can be traced to the multiplying and infinitely more complex tasks the civil service is expected to perform. It is one thing to ask that public employees build roads or deliver mail; it is quite another to mandate that they ensure adequate levels of health care for older and poor citizens, or that they clean the environment of hazardous materials. Since the New Deal, many government jobs and many government employees have been concerned with such tasks.

Guidance in identifying specific problems to be solved and specific populations to be served has generally been provided by legislation notable for its turgid prose and murky objectives. Problem solving and policy implementation in this context have proceeded with ever-increasing oversight and micromanagement from Congress. This obviously contributes new tasks to the bureaucratic mix, redefines others, and adds another dimension to definitions of efficient and effective bureaucratic performance.

At its heart, however, the problem of merit remains a problem of politics and of consensus about what a merit system should be. The balance between the president and Congress and between both and the bureaucracy is critical but still tenuous. In the past, the character of the public service mirrored widely held political views and values.[4] At the present, even identifying what the pattern of those views might be is difficult. Certainly the nature of the candidacy of Ross Perot, the presidential election in 1992, and the congressional elections in 1994 cast doubt on the existence of a positive and widely shared view of government. If government itself is the target, what is to become of its most visible artifact?

This does not suggest that no change is possible in an atmosphere of generalized distrust of government. Rather, it should point to the profound need for real changes that will permit government institutions and employees to function as problem solvers and partners in governing. For that to occur, the lessons of the past must be integrated into consideration of the future. It can be argued that Nelson's "grand irony" is supported by a set of harsh realities about both politics and merit. These realities have generally been absent in discussions of reform.

Harsh Reality #1: For Public Organizations, Being Controlled Does Not Mean Being Effective

Past efforts directed at improved responsiveness (read political control) or efficiency have consistently resulted in additional rules and regulations. Planning, programming, and budgeting, management by objective, and performance appraisal all added new paperwork. Even the Civil Service Reform Act added new rules and procedures to the existing base. This has continued to obfuscate accountability and to decrease the ability of elected officials to understand bureaucratic activity, much less direct it. Because the emphasis was on reform through increased short-term *control,* rather than increased long-term *capacity,* the ability of the civil service to perform new tasks and to assume new responsibilities could not meet reformers' expectations.

Efforts directed at management improvements have often met the same fate. In the presence of a rule- and constraint-laden system, the authority, flexibility, and discretion necessary for effective management have either not been created or not been developed. The civil service system has not been about management; it has been about the exclusion of undesirable influences (defined differently throughout its history) and about control. To a considerable extent, it still is. Absent a positive overall vision for the public service and public management, the present system has developed with an essentially negative view of each. Absent a clear set of political and managerial objectives, and a clear understanding of how the system really works, reforms have awarded discretion in the wrong places and at the wrong times. They have served to constrain the wrong people in the wrong ways. The Senior Executive Service is one example; its members, the most talented men and women in the career service, have often been isolated from key decisions, from important policy discussions, and from the trust, respect, and authority central to effective management.

For reform to be successful, it is necessary for reformers to understand the management implications of reform and change, to prepare managers for the new challenges, and to give them the authority and flexibility to meet those challenges. Of equal importance, it is necessary to ensure that members of the public service are accountable for their *performance,* not for simple adherence to rules and regulations.

Past efforts at reform, whatever their intent, have not changed the base, but have operated at the fringes of the system. Jimmy Carter's "comprehensive" effort did not significantly affect the base of unreformed classification, compensation, and procedural complexity. That base continued to perform as it had for a century; the various components of the reform were confounded by it. The base itself must be the target in the future.

Harsh Reality #2: Not All Public Organizations Are Alike; Reform Will Have a Differential Impact

Chapter 7 described both the changing nature of government work and the changing workforce. The message is simple and straightforward: traditional notions about government employment and the tasks public employees undertake are badly outdated and cannot serve as guidelines for change and reform. Conjuring visions of "seas of faceless bureaucrats" may be good political rhetoric, but it does not describe the reality of many agencies.

Further, change has never occurred through some magical process. It is difficult, it is painful, and it takes a long time. Public organizations are no different from any others in requiring both the proper circumstances for change and adequate time in which to achieve it. Meeting these conditions in the public sector is no easy task, but understanding that government organizations are different and do not all do the same things is an important starting point. It is equally important to recognize that not all have the same capacity for change, not necessarily because some organizations decide to resist, but because public organizations have different structures, functions, environments, resources, and histories.

Public Organizations Vary by Size and Structure

Bureaucratic size and structure vary among government organizations. Even in large bureaucratic departments, there are smaller, more flexible units. Increasingly, the service-delivery function has been contracted out and small numbers of government employees manage larger numbers of contractors. Professional networks, rather than formal structures and organizations, are emerging as critical realities in the public sector.

All these variations will have an effect on reform. Reforming fundamental governmental processes in government organizations will have less impact in agencies that depend heavily on contracting out, for example. The basic mission of some organizations has been altered, often inadvertently, by decisions made about contracting out. Core organizational activities may now occur outside the organizations. Decisions about what should be contracted out have also been short-term and frequently financial rather than mission based, and have virtually never been connected to a discussion of overall agency effectiveness.

At the same time, traditional relationships have been dramatically altered by the emerging pattern of third-party management. As Donald Kettl has observed, the intricate web of relationships created by the sharing of power defies standard categories of public or private power and responsibility.[5] Further, it suggests strongly that effective strategies for change and reform must proceed from a full understanding of the interrelated networks of responsibilities, rather than from the more usual perspective of public/private difference and separation. The authority and control of government agencies and employees are eroded in important ways; the accountability for government action, however, is unaltered.

Public Organizations Vary by Function

Tasks and functions range from the relatively simple (processing payments) to the highly complex (disposing of radioactive waste). These differences shape opportunities for change. In addition, however, it is necessary to consider in a different way the dimensions by which organizations vary. Function, for example, must take on a new meaning.

The history of civil service classification is one of narrow definition of task, of job, and of purpose. What difference each makes—and, in fact, whether they are related—has rarely been an issue. In such a climate, efforts to connect function and process to results have often been futile. The General Accounting Office reported in 1992, for example, that although two-thirds of the 103 federal agencies surveyed had strategic plans, only nine indicated that those plans were related to intended results.[6]

The simple performance of a task or the following of the correct procedure was the norm for evaluation of both individual and organizational performance. No one asked, "So what?" Future reforms must encourage that question and reward employees who ask it. Function and process must be considered with, integrated into, and substantively linked to both management and the achievement of goals.

Internal Processes Differ

"Process" must also be rethought. The term has assumed a pejorative flavor in relation to government activities: the mindless linking of unnecessary procedures into broader sets of unnecessary processes. The National Performance Review quoted an employee who argued that "in government, process is our most important product."[7] The *linking* of process and product, however, creates a different definition of the term; processes become critical activities that must be performed effectively if the organization is to meet its goals and objectives. Identification of core processes and support of them through the creation of systems that facilitate their smooth operation have been notably absent in past reforms of the merit system.

Linking process to product in future reforms will require two sets of activities. First, agencies themselves must conduct serious audits of their internal operating processes. Most of these processes have grown incrementally over time and many have little current relevance to the effective operation of the organizations. Organizations such as the Internal Revenue Service, which have already conducted such internal analyses, are dramatically reducing and simplifying both processes and systems. The IRS is moving from an organization that operated with twelve basic units, for example, to one with five "business systems."[8] Indeed, some current prescriptions for organizational change advocate "blowing up" existing systems and starting from scratch.[9] While that is probably neither possible nor desirable for most public organizations, the searching analysis that it suggests is fundamental to effective performance.

Second, civil service systems and processes must be viewed both in terms of individual agency activities and in a larger government-wide context. Human-resource management is an important part of government, but it is only one part among many. It acts in tandem with other key systems, such as those concerning budgets, financial management, and information management. These systems, too, are prime contenders for major overhauls and improved coordination with other management activities. Reforming one without changing the others, however, is throwing good money after bad.

Previous Experiences with Reform and Change Differ
An additional dimension of variation is provided by an examination of the ways in which agencies have previously dealt with problems and challenges. Some organizations have been public leaders and have undertaken large-scale reforms essentially on their own. Those organizations committed to reengineering, for example, are well into major change processes. In those organizations, flexibility and innovation are already valued; organizational leaders have demonstrated that they are willing to take risks in the interest of better performance and higher standards.

Other organizations are not so well positioned for change. Agencies that have existed in the most turbulent environments and that have been subject to large budget or staff reductions need to regain some internal balance and coherence before additional changes are possible. Constant change and turmoil are debilitating. The Department of Housing and Urban Development, for example, saw its basic mission, as well as its budget and staff, attacked for more than a decade. Both mission and commitment need to be restored before constructive internal change can occur. The bunker mentality created by consistent external onslaught and the bureaucrat bashing of the 1970s and 1980s does not go away overnight; its presence virtually ensures that new efforts at change and reform will fail. That is one of the enduring lessons of the Civil Service Reform Act of 1978.[10]

Leadership Qualities and Capacities Differ

Still other public organizations do not have the leadership or managerial capabilities to undertake successful change. Leading change, particularly in an environment characterized by multiple and conflicting responsibilities, is enormously risky and challenging. There is little in the content or history of the civil service system that has valued or consciously developed management skills and capacities; still less has risk taking been encouraged. Those public managers who do choose to be managers of change characterize their activity as "life on the edge." [11] If their commitment to improved performance is to continue, something must reinforce or reward their effort. They must also know that they have the freedom to fail, but still to be viewed as effective managers.

Shared political/career leadership adds another critical dimension of uncertainty to the potential for change. The political management strategies detailed in chapter 6 do not begin from an assumption of partnership and shared interests. Rather, most assume a confrontational stance directed toward *forcing* change. This is problematic in two ways: first, the strategy creates a top-down model of change that conflicts with models of successful change processes; second, the short tenure of many political appointees attenuates their potential for being effective leaders in the reform effort.

The Ability to Sustain Change Differs

It is now acknowledged that creating real change in large organizations is a long-term process. Most private-sector executives who describe the activity in their organizations discuss it in terms of a five-to seven-year time frame.[12] Private-sector executives and theorists who address change also consistently emphasize the critical role played by leadership. Without the total commitment of top leaders, they argue, effective change is not likely to occur. For public organizations, the lesson is that leadership must be a partnership between political and career executives; organizations in which that partnership is forged will be the most receptive to reform and will be the most likely to implement reform measures effectively. Bluntly put, career executives have to be part of the change team simply because they will be around longer.

In this context, successful change and reform will be a multilevel process: a fostering and development of organizational leadership, a stabilization and strengthening of the organizations through effective leadership, the creation of a clear model of effective change in public organizations using success in other public organizations as a referent, and a design of reform that fits agency needs and purposes as well as government-wide ones. Under these circumstances, *all* public organizations can change, but providing the necessary conditions lengthens the process even further.

Harsh Reality #3: Changes Already Underway in Public Organizations Have Altered the Rules of the Game for the Civil Service and for Reformers

The discussion in chapter 7 described the dramatically changed nature of much public work: complex problem solving on the frontier of knowledge, the demand for more expertise in the right places, the need for smart buyers and good contract managers, and the need to make the most of the opportunities that increased diversity in the workforce will offer. The challenges presented by these shifts from tradition are already being addressed by many organizations.

At the same time, new approaches to management are causing significant alterations to traditional patterns of communication and decision making inside the organizations. Some of these approaches have important implications for how the organizations will deal with future change, as well as for the way in which the organizations relate, or do not relate, to citizens, elected officials, and others in their environments.

The most important of these management philosophies is total quality management, or TQM. The principles of TQM are in clear contrast to the hierarchical methods of the traditional civil service. Four of the most important are (1) a focus on product, rather than process; (2) a focus on the customer; (3) the elimination or redefinition of middle management, and (4) the empowerment of workers, which entails devolution of authority and group problem solving.[13] Communication becomes multidirectional. The emphasis on groups and teams spans formal organizational boundaries and procedures. The absence or significant reduction of the cadre of middle managers turns hierarchical control on its head. In many respects, the new manager is a facilitator and an equal, rather than an authority figure. Most federal organizations now have quality-improvement programs. The fundamental concepts associated with TQM are not only accepted, but are being implemented in many places at all levels of government.

How does the redefinition of internal processes change the rules of the game outside the organization? The first major change is in the relationship of the organization and its employees to the citizen as customer. The focus on product and customer satisfaction gives the customer—the citizen—a voice in the organization that has not been present before. It effectively destroys the inequalities produced by rules and regulations and by the unilateral nature of bureaucratic power and control.

On the other hand, the concept of customer satisfaction is necessarily defined in a different way in the public sector. There are, for example, many diverse customers, rather than an easily identified single customer or set of customers. Customers of public organizations include the actual recipients of services delivered by the organizations; they also include all the actors in the political arena: elected officials, interest groups, the media, other public organizations, and other citizens. For some large organizations, such as the Internal Revenue Service, which are part of much larger departments, the customer includes those larger departments as well.

To complicate matters further, citizens relate to public organizations in different and sometimes conflicting ways. DiIulio, Garvey, and Kettl provide four possible perspectives.[14] Citizens will be service recipients of one or more public organizations. As such, they will be concerned about both quality and responsiveness; that is, they will want the organizations to be responsive to their specific concerns and demands. Citizens will relate to some public organizations as partners in service provision; they will serve as advisors, as contractors, or as co-providers. In that capacity, they will tend to evaluate the relationship in terms of the effectiveness of the organizations. Citizens will also relate to public organizations as general overseers of performance; that is, they will be concerned about the accountability of the organizations and their employees. Finally, citizens will relate to *all* public organizations as taxpayers and will view them from the perspective of efficiency. These multiple perspectives will clearly produce different evaluations of bureaucratic performance and different remedies for bureaucratic problems. The differences may not be reconcilable.

Even if public organizations are successful in clarifying who their customers are, therefore, the public context creates new dimensions of complexity. Because these dimensions are part of the organizations' activities and responsibilities, they are now also part of any consideration of future reform. The reform process will be more open, more multidimensional, and more subject to conflicting perspectives.

Harsh Reality #4: Creating Multiple Accountability Mechanisms Does Not Increase Accountability

For much of the history of the merit system, dissatisfaction with government performance and accountability has resulted in the creation of additional rules and legal constraints. Both the president and the Congress have expanded their efforts to achieve more direction and control in the past two decades. The resulting maze has been termed the "baggage of merit," which does not "clarify and define, but obscures." [15]

Despite the long academic debate about the relative power of internal versus external mechanisms for ensuring accountability,[16] the emphasis in reality has been on external, hierarchical, and legal mechanisms. Presidential direction through political appointees, congressional supervision through micromanagement and hearings, and judicial oversight are examples, as are the rules and regulations administered hierarchically within the organizations.

Barbara Romzek and Melvin Dubnick note, however, that these are only a limited part of the total set of potential mechanisms, and that they are probably not the most effective ones. Arguing that accountability mechanisms vary along two dimensions—source of control and degree of control—they identify four categories of such mechanisms in public organizations. Each emphasizes different values and different processes. Bureaucratic mechanisms are essentially internal and emphasize efficiency. Legal accountability mechanisms are external and reflect an emphasis on the rule of law; professional accountability is both internal and individual and the primary value is expertise. Political accountability is external but sporadic and values responsiveness.[17] Romzek and Dubnick observe that

> each of the four types of accountability mechanisms is equally legitimate, and all may be present simultaneously. . . . Ironically, when more than one type of accountability system is active, individuals and agencies may have some de-

gree of influence on the type of accountability mechanisms most frequently used. The choices made under these circumstances are at the very heart of the tasks of "management" in public agencies.[18]

Thus, the emphasis on multiple mechanisms, and on ever-increasing numbers of them, not only creates a more complex set of tasks for public managers, but increases their discretion in important ways.

The need for increased managerial flexibility and discretion that is inherent in new management philosophies and reforms differs dramatically from the essentially negative discretion described above, but the differences need to be carefully delineated. Simplified accountability mechanisms, and consensus about which are most appropriate and dominant, would permit the positive transfer of authority and discretion to managers. As Romzek and Dubnick observe, effective reforms must generally move from bureaucratic and legalistic accountability mechanisms toward those that emphasize trust and outcomes.[19] The "entrepreneurial government" reforms now on the table emphasize the latter. Quite clearly, however, they challenge the tradition.

It is important to note, as well, that the emphasis of TQM on employee empowerment and participation places a high value on informal group and individual accountability mechanisms. These are internal to the group or to the individual and are closely associated with ethically responsible behavior. Although there is a literature that suggests that commitment to the public service can serve a motivational purpose for many public employees, the relationship between that commitment and public accountability is less often explored.[20] It is precisely that link, however, that will be an important part of reforms that emphasize discretion and outcomes, rather than process and control.

Harsh Reality #5: Merit and Management Reforms Have Serious Implications for Governance

Just as many past reforms have been at the fringes of the merit system, most have been sold as technical adjustments. The assumption has been that the base was solid, and tinkering would fix whatever problems had been identified. The pay-for-performance reforms associated with the CSRA are one example of this pattern. They were described as a technical improvement to management systems; their intent was to increase productivity and efficiency.

In fact, many of the components of pay for performance challenge fundamental tenets of the civil service system. The move away from standardized treatment of employees to managerial discretion and differential reward clearly suggests a public manager with substantial authority and flexibility, and one quite different from the constrained, rule-driven administrator commonly associated with the civil service.[21] Such a manager will behave differently both inside and outside the organization.

Further, if pay for performance were to work as the theory associated with it suggests, it would link individual performance to the overall attainment of organizational objectives—to the effective pursuit of public policy. That is why both public organizations and the civil service exist. It is the point of reforms that focus on outcomes and on customer satisfaction. But the extension of that point, and the connection between the pursuit of these objectives in public organizations and the quality of government and governance, is often not made. It should be.

Members of the civil service represent the single most visible link between the government and the citizens. How well the merit system serves its members is directly related to how well those members serve citizens. The values inherent in the system are reflected in the efforts, attitudes, and behavior of its members and, therefore, in the quality of government and governance. The fit between values that the polity deems it desirable to pursue and those reflected in its public service is critically important, but the casting of reform in technical terms removes that fit from the debate.

This returns again to the theme stressed throughout this book: the intricate relationship between politics and merit and the foundation for merit that politics must provide. The debate described above is political; its outcome can only be determined in the political arena. The fundamental legitimacy and effectiveness of merit is based, and must be pursued, in that arena as well.

Harsh Reality #6: Continued Reliance on Private-Sector Reform Models Ignores Important Lessons from the Public Sector

The idea of borrowing public management reforms from the private sector is nearly as old as the civil service itself. Transplanting private techniques essentially intact into public organizations was, and is, considered the path to improved productivity and efficiency. Scientific management, planning, programming, budgeting, management by objective, pay for performance, and TQM were all such transplants.

There are lessons to be learned from private-sector techniques and experience. There are also, however, lessons to be learned from excellent *public* organizations, and those lessons have been far more rare in the reform tradition. Organizations such as the Internal Revenue Service, many agencies in the Department of Defense, and the Forest Service have a long tradition of creative and farsighted management. Their experiences with change and with the translation of other models of change to a public context can provide guidelines for other public organizations. Why have they not?

There are at least two reasons and they are related. First, examples of excellence and effective change in public organizations are not widely known and disseminated. Even when they are identified, they are rarely the subject of the in-depth case analyses common to those private organizations judged to be excellent and high performing.

This is due, at least in part, to the perception of many public executives that publicity or attention to their efforts to change their organizations would bring political scrutiny at critical stages of the change process. Case studies of reengineering and other management reforms in two large agencies demonstrated that, in both, potential congressional involvement was perceived by top managers to be a negative influence and one that would likely stop the change processes cold.[22]

This has important implications for change in public organizations and for leaders who will implement that change. The former is most significant: those organizations that have successfully moved to new management methods and styles have done so under conditions not found in many private firms. How they did it and what they learned should be a part of the public-reform tradition.

Conclusion: The Elements of Transformation

The need for change is well established. Although the system is out of date, however, the concept of merit is not. It is necessary clearly to draw the line between the *baggage* of merit and the essentially sound principles that the system should support government wide. The need for a public management system that is fair and equitable, that addresses issues of recruiting, rewarding, and managing a committed and qualified workforce, and that serves the public and elected officials productively and effectively remains central to good government.

So, too, does the compass that Kettl advocates. There is a long tradition in the United States of swinging from centralization to decentralization and back again. The velocity of the swings can be attenuated, however, by careful attention to what must remain at the center when decentralization occurs—what values and principles *must* be retained, maintained, and advocated. This should define the role of the Office of Personnel Management or whatever succeeds it. That agency must see itself as a partner in good management and good government; it must reach out to federal organizations and their managers and support them in their complicated efforts for change.

There is no question that the merit system of the future will operate in a different environment. Economic resources will be more limited, tasks will be ever more diverse and complex, organizations will be smaller and more open to both employee and citizen participation. The focus on product and on producing something that works for those outside the organizations is already changing internal functions and processes for many public organizations.

The dilemma will be to provide the necessary expertise and management capacity, as well as the discretion and authority to use them well, while also creating and maintaining internal and external accountability mechanisms that support the legitimacy of the merit system. That means gaining and retaining the political support fundamental to a positive role.

This has always been the conundrum of merit. Politics had to be both included in and excluded from the system during its early years; it still does. Balancing the values that this byzantine equation required has often been the primary activity, rather than the foundation, of the merit system. That is why simplified accountability will be an important part of the new foundation of merit. The employees and the managers the system supports must have the freedom and discretion to make timely and necessary decisions and to try new approaches without fear of punitive response. They must have the freedom to fail and to learn from their mistakes, not to cover them and retreat to the safety of boundaries, rules, and hierarchy. They must also be held accountable for their performance and that of their organizations.

New reforms must focus on management and management systems, not as neutral, technical artifacts, but as critical components of an effective policy process. Just as politics must support merit, an effective merit system must support and implement political decisions. If a hierarchical model of political direction ever worked, that time is past. The relationships among the public service, the president, and Congress must reflect shared goals, communication about the real issues, and joint participation in critical decisions.

Further, new reforms must focus on broad components of management and merit. The narrow focus and limited definitions of past efforts made a major contribution to the complexity of the present system. Both simplicity and comprehensiveness can be achieved by a clear statement of purpose, by careful analysis of the processes and systems necessary to support that purpose, and by a clear linking of the two. Flexibility, innovation, and better problem solving emerge from such systems; they are not nurtured in rigid boxes.

All of this suggests a profoundly redefined attitude toward the public service and its members. It is not possible to provide the flexibility necessary for the future in a system that does not have confidence in the public service. Accountability will necessarily reside to an increasing extent with individual members and managers; that means loosening controls, encouraging risk, permitting mistakes, and building trust. If the first manager who makes a mistake in a new system is punished and pulled back, the reform will not succeed. Creation of a "trust cushion" is key.

In the final analysis, therefore, a revitalized system of merit depends as much on the existence of a supportive environment that reinforces its activities as on the introduction of new reforms and management systems. The most excellent managers in the world—and there are many in the public service—falter in an atmosphere of consistent suspicion and distrust. Like government itself, the vitality of the public service rests on a foundation of trust, respect, and the ability to pursue common goals effectively. In that endeavor, politics and merit cannot be separate and exclusive spheres; discovery of the historically elusive common ground is the starting point for reform. This is the hardest, but the most important, lesson from the past and consideration for the future. The past need not be prologue in this regard; we can, and should, learn from it.

A prominent part of that learning must be that public service reforms are not merely technical, nor are they tangential to other policy changes. The most carefully designed policies and programs will fail if they are not successfully implemented. Effective implementation and effective government depend on an effective, respected, and committed public service. That vision for future reforms will build a firmer foundation, not only for merit, but for government as well.

Notes

Chapter One: Civil Service Systems and Government

1. Dwight Waldo, *The Administrative State* (New York: Ronald Press, 1948).

2. See, for example, Stephen Skowronek, *Building a New American State: The Expansion of National Administrative Capacities, 1877–1920* (New York: Cambridge University Press, 1982); Michael Nelson, "A Short, Ironic History of American National Bureaucracy," *Journal of Politics* 44 (August 1982): 747–78; and Patricia W. Ingraham and David H. Rosenbloom, "The New Public Personnel and the New Public Service," *Public Administration Review* 49 (March–April 1989): 116–25.

3. Nelson, "Short, Ironic History," 749.

4. For a thorough discussion of this issue, see G. Calvin Mackenzie, ed., *The In-and-Outers: Presidential Appointees and Transient Government in Washington* (Baltimore: Johns Hopkins University Press, 1987), and Patricia W. Ingraham, "Building Bridges or Burning Them? The President, the Appointees, and the Bureaucracy," *Public Administration Review* 47 (September–October 1987): 425–35.

5. Frederick C. Mosher, *Democracy and the Public Service* (New York: Oxford University Press, 1968), 55.

6. See, for example, Leonard White's classic works on the early governments; see also Skowronek, *Building a New American State,* and Patricia W. Ingraham and David H. Rosenbloom, "Political Foundations of the American Federal Service: Rebuilding a Crumbling Base," *Public Administration Review* 50 (March–April 1990): 210–19.

7. For a discussion of bureaucratic rules, see Herbert Kaufman, *Red Tape* (Washington, D.C.: Brookings Institution, 1977), and Kenneth J. Meier, *Politics and the Bureaucracy: Policymaking in the Fourth Branch of Government,* 3d ed. (Pacific Grove, Calif.: Brooks/Cole, 1993).

8. For a full discussion of reform in Western democracies, see Patricia W. Ingraham, "The Reform Agenda: A Comparative Perspective," and John Halligan, "The Diffusion of Reform," in *Comparative Civil Service Reform,* edited by Hans Bekke, James Perry, and Theo Toonen (Bloomington: Indiana University Press, 1995).

9. See H. H. Gerth and C. Wright Mills, eds., *From Max Weber: Essays in Sociology* (New York: Oxford University Press, 1976), part 2.

10. See the discussion in Waldo, *Administrative State,* and Harold Seidman

and Robert Gilmour, *Politics, Position, and Power: From the Positive to the Regulatory State,* 4th ed. (New York: Oxford University Press, 1986).

11. See the arguments, for example, in Charles Goodsell, *The Case for Bureaucracy,* 2d ed. (Chatham, N.J.: Chatham House, 1985).

12. Ibid., 329.

13. Theodore J. Lowi, *The End of Liberalism* (New York: Norton, 1979).

14. For discussion on this point, see Meier, *Politics and the Bureaucracy,* and B. Guy Peters, *The American Public Policy Process* (Chatham, N.J.: Chatham House, 1991).

15. See the discussion in Peters, *American Public Policy Process.*

16. See Randall B. Ripley and Grace A. Franklin, *Congress, the Bureaucracy, and Public Policy* (Chicago: Dorsey Press, 1987).

17. Woodrow Wilson, "The Study of Administration," *Political Science Quarterly* 2 (June 1887): 200; for a more contemporary interpretation, see Jameson W. Doig, " 'If I See a Murderous Fellow Sharpening a Knife Cleverly. . .': The Wilsonian Dichotomy and the Public Authority Tradition," *Public Administration Review* 43 (March–April 1983): 292–304.

18. Mosher, *Democracy and the Public Service,* 3. For a more recent discussion of the same issues, see "Forum on Public Administration and the Constitution," *Public Administration Review* 53 (May–June 1993): 237–67.

19. See Waldo, *Administrative State;* John A. Rohr, *To Run a Constitution* (Lawrence: University of Kansas Press, 1986); and David H. Rosenbloom and James D. Carroll, *Toward Constitutional Competence* (Englewood Cliffs, N.J.: Prentice-Hall, 1989).

20. See, for example, Ezra N. Suliemau, ed., *Bureaucrats and Policy Making* (New York: Holmes and Meier, 1984), and Joel D. Aberbach, Robert D. Putnam, and Bert A. Rockman, *Bureaucrats and Politicians in Western Democracies* (Cambridge, Mass.: Harvard University Press, 1981).

21. See the discussion of Great Britain in Donald Savoie, *Reagan, Thatcher, and Mulroney* (Pittsburgh: University of Pittsburgh Press, 1994).

22. Donald J. Devine, "Political Administration: The Right Way," in *Steering the Elephant: How Washington Works,* edited by Robert Rector and Michael Sanera (New York: Universe Books, 1987), 129.

23. See National Performance Review, *Creating a Government that Works Better and Costs Less: Report of the National Performance Review* (Washington, D.C.: U.S. Government Printing Office, 1993).

24. Luther Gulick and Lyndall Urwick, eds., *Papers on the Science of Administration* (New York: Institute of Public Administration, 1937), 100.

25. See "Report of the President's Committee on Administrative Management," in *Basic Documents of American Public Administration, 1776–1950,* edited by Frederick C. Mosher (New York: Holmes and Meier, 1976), 110–38.

26. Herbert Kaufman, "Administrative Decentralization and Political Power," in *Current Issues in Public Administration,* edited by Frederick Lane, 2d ed. (New York: St. Martin's Press, 1978), 462–76.

27. Wilson, "Study of Administration," 201.

28. See, for example, the arguments advanced by Waldo in *Administrative*

State and those of Paul Appleby in *Policy and Administration* (University: University of Alabama Press, 1949).

29. David Osborne and Ted Gaebler, *Reinventing Government: How the Entrepreneurial Spirit Is Transforming the Public Sector* (Reading, Mass.: Addison-Wesley, 1992).

30. For a discussion of Congress in this regard, see David H. Rosenbloom and Bernard H. Ross, "Administrative Theory, Political Power, and Government Reform," in *New Paradigms for Government: Issues for the Changing Public Service,* edited by Patricia W. Ingraham, Barbara Romzek, and Associates (San Francisco: Jossey-Bass, 1994), 145–67.

31. See the discussion in James W. Fesler and Donald F. Kettl, *The Politics of the Administrative Process* (Chatham, N.J.: Chatham House, 1991). Chapter 7 is an excellent summary discussion of the issues related to political appointments. The data cited here are from that source.

32. David K. Hamilton, "The Staffing Function in Illinois State Government after Rutan," *Public Administration Review* 53 (July–August 1993): 382.

33. See the discussion in Fesler and Kettl, *Politics of the Administrative Process,* 138–40.

34. Peter M. Benda and David H. Rosenbloom, "The Hatch Act and the Contemporary Public Service," in *Agenda for Excellence: Public Service in America,* edited by Patricia W. Ingraham and Donald F. Kettl (Chatham, N.J.: Chatham House, 1992), 25.

35. National Academy of Public Administration, *Leading People in Change: Empowerment, Commitment, Accountability* (Washington, D.C.: National Academy of Public Administration, 1993), vii.

36. B. Guy Peters and Donald Savoie, "Governance in a Changing Environment" (Canadian Centre for Management Development, Ottawa, 1993, manuscript), 2.

37. Patricia W. Ingraham, "Of Pigs in Pokes and Policy Diffusion: Another Look at Pay for Performance," *Public Administration Review* 53 (July–August 1993): 348–56.

38. See Patricia W. Ingraham and B. Guy Peters, "The Conundrum of Reform: A Comparative Analysis," *Review of Public Personnel Administration* 8 (Summer 1988): 3–16.

39. Peters and Savoie, "Governance in a Changing Environment," 5.

40. Charles H. Levine, "The Federal Government in the Year 2000," in Ingraham and Kettl, *Agenda for Excellence,* 182. The term "intellectual deficit" is also from Levine.

Chapter Two: The Origins of the Merit System

1. Francis E. Rourke, "Whose Bureaucracy Is This, Anyway? Congress, the President, and Public Administration," *PS: Political Science and Politics* 26 (December 1993): 687.

2. Ibid.

3. Philip Kurland, "Reflections on Process and the Constitution," *University*

of Chicago Magazine 69 (1976): 7. For additional discussions of administration and the Constitution, see David H. Rosenbloom, *Public Administration and the Law* (New York: Marcel Dekker, 1983), and Rohr, *To Run a Constitution.*

4. Alexander Hamilton, "Federalist No. 68," in *The Federalist Papers,* edited by Clinton Rossiter (New York: Mentor, 1961), 414.

5. For an excellent discussion of the two men's views, see Lynton K. Caldwell, *The Administrative Theories of Hamilton and Jefferson* (Chicago: University of Chicago Press, 1944). See also Louis C. Gawthrop, *The Administrative Process and Democratic Theory* (Boston: Houghton Mifflin, 1970), chapter 2.

6. James Madison, "Federalist No. 51," in Rossiter, *Federalist Papers,* 322.

7. Wilson, "Study of Administration," 200.

8. Mosher, *Democracy and the Public Service,* 55; see also chapter 3 for a discussion of the evolution of the American civil service. Please note that for the early period of development, I use the terms "public service" and "civil service" interchangeably, although a formal civil service was not created until 1883.

9. For conflicting views on the call and duty of public service, see Lloyd G. Nigro and William D. Richardson, "The Founders' Unsentimental View of Public Service in the American Regime," in Ingraham and Kettl, *Agenda for Excellence,* 3–24, and David K. Hart, "The Virtuous Citizen, the Honorable Bureaucrat, and 'Public' Administration," *Public Administration Review* 44 (March–April 1984): 111–19.

10. See Carl R. Fish, *The Civil Service and the Patronage* (Cambridge, Mass.: Harvard University Press, 1904).

11. Mosher reports that of about 3,000 federal civilian employees in 1800, only about 150 were in Washington. See Mosher, *Democracy and the Public Service,* 58.

12. The term is taken from U.S. Civil Service Commission, *Biography of an Ideal: A History of the Federal Civil Service* (Washington, D.C.: U.S. Civil Service Commission, 1973), 12.

13. Leonard D. White, *The Jeffersonians: A Study in Administrative History, 1801–1829* (New York: Macmillan, 1951), 349.

14. See Paul P. Van Riper, *History of the United States Civil Service* (Evanston, Ill.: Row, Peterson, 1958), 24.

15. See Mosher, *Democracy and the Public Service,* 59–61, and Sidney H. Aronson, *Status and Kinship in the Higher Civil Service* (Cambridge, Mass.: Harvard University Press, 1964), for a discussion of the numbers of appointees and their socioeconomic backgrounds.

16. White, *Jeffersonians,* 549.

17. Ibid., 130.

18. Mosher, *Democracy and the Public Service,* 60.

19. The term is Mosher's; see ibid., 62.

20. Leonard D. White, *The Jacksonians: A Study in Administrative History, 1829–1861* (New York: Macmillan, 1954), 14.

21. Ibid., 332.

22. Fish, *Civil Service,* 125. A different number is provided by Erik Eriksson,

whose analysis concluded that Jackson removed about 919 of a total of 10,093 federal employees, or one out of eleven. See Erik McKinley Eriksson, "The Federal Civil Service under President Jackson," *Mississippi Valley Historical Review* 13 (March 1927): 517–40.

23. U.S. Civil Service Commission, *Biography of an Ideal*, 24.

24. Ibid., 26.

25. Fish, *Civil Service*, 171.

26. U.S. Civil Service Commission, *Biography of an Ideal*, 28.

27. Ibid., 29.

28. Leonard D. White, *The Republican Era: A Study in Administrative History, 1869–1901* (New York: Macmillan, 1958), 191.

29. Mosher, *Democracy and the Public Service*, 63. Mosher concludes that spoils created a system that was neither responsive nor responsible to the citizenry.

30. White, *Jacksonians*, 362.

31. Fish, *Civil Service*, 209.

32. U.S. Civil Service Commission, *Biography of an Ideal*, 30.

33. Ibid.

34. Ibid., 33.

35. Van Riper, *History*, 229.

36. Mosher, *Democracy and the Public Service*, 65.

37. U.S Civil Service Commission, *Biography of an Ideal*, 37.

38. White, *Republican Era*, 6.

39. *Harpers Weekly*, October 1, 1881, quoted in U. S. Civil Service Commission, *Biography of an Ideal*, 39.

40. U.S. Civil Service Commission, *Biography of an Ideal*, 43.

41. Van Riper, *History*, 105.

42. Mosher, *Democracy and the Public Service*, 70.

Chapter Three: The Evolution of the Merit System

1. Dorman B. Eaton, *Civil Service in Great Britain* (New York: Harper and Bros., 1879), 403.

2. U.S. Civil Service Commission, *Biography of an Ideal*, 46.

3. Ibid., 48.

4. "Blanketing in" is the practice of bringing offices that were previously patronage positions into the competitive service. Although the patronage appointees who hold the jobs when they are blanketed in are not required to take an examination to hold the positions, all future appointments must follow merit hiring procedures.

5. U.S. Civil Service Commission, *Biography of an Ideal*, 49.

6. Nelson, "Short, Ironic History," 767.

7. Frank Mann Stewart, *The National Civil Service Reform League: History, Activities, and Problems* (Austin: University of Texas Press, 1929), 101.

8. Ibid., 103.

9. The concept of a politics-administration dichotomy continues to be a hotly

debated topic in contemporary public administration. For thorough analyses of both the early writers and contemporary interpretations, see Waldo, *Administrative State,* and Doig, " 'If I See a Murderous Fellow. . .'" For a perspective that argues that the dichotomy does and should exist, see Michael Sanera, "Implementing the Mandate," in *Mandate for Leadership II: Continuing the Conservative Revolution,* edited by Stuart Butler, Michael Sanera, and W. Bruce Weinrod (Washington, D.C.: Heritage Foundation, 1984), 560–99.

10. Wilson, "Study of Administration," 201, 209–10.

11. Peri E. Arnold, *Making the Managerial Presidency: Comprehensive Reorganization Planning, 1905–1980* (Princeton: Princeton University Press, 1986), 20.

12. Ronald C. Moe, *The Hoover Commissions Revisited* (Boulder, Colo.: Westview Press, 1982), 8.

13. Van Riper, *History,* 234.

14. General Charles G. Dawes, quoted in Gawthrop, *Administrative Process and Democratic Theory,* 93–96.

15. An earlier Pay and Classification Act had been passed in 1853, but it covered only departmental clerks. See White, *Jacksonians,* 391.

16. Classification Act of 1923, excerpted in Mosher, *Basic Documents of American Public Administration,* 100–102.

17. Ibid., 100.

18. Cited in Van Riper, *History,* 304.

19. Lucius Wilmerding, Jr., *Government by Merit* (New York: McGraw-Hill, 1935), 57.

20. For an in-depth discussion of classification and its current status, see U.S. Merit Systems Protection Board, *OPM's Classification and Qualification Systems: A Renewed Emphasis, A Changing Perspective* (Washington, D.C.: U.S. Merit Systems Protection Board, 1989).

21. Stewart, *National Civil Service Reform League,* 177.

22. Fesler and Kettl, *Politics of the Administrative Process,* 117.

23. Noncompetitive or unassembled examinations are essentially thorough reviews of credentials or previous experience.

24. Fesler and Kettl, *Politics of the Administrative Process,* 225.

25. U.S. Civil Service Commission, *Biography of an Ideal,* 64.

26. Mosher, *Democracy and the Public Service,* 79.

27. See James A. Medeiros and David E. Schmitt, *Public Bureaucracy: Values and Perspectives* (North Scituate, Mass.: Duxbury Press, 1977).

28. Van Riper, *History,* 315.

29. Herbert Kaufman, "The Growth of the Federal Personnel System," in *The Federal Government Service,* by the American Assembly (New York: Columbia University Press, 1954), 39.

30. See U.S. Civil Service Commission, *Biography of an Ideal,* 67–70.

31. Rowland Egger, "The Period of Crisis: 1933 to 1945," in *American Public Administration: Past, Present, and Future,* edited by Frederick C. Mosher (University: University of Alabama Press, 1975), 71.

32. "Report of the President's Committee," 113–14.

33. Arnold, *Making the Managerial Presidency*, 117.

34. Benda and Rosenbloom, "Hatch Act," 25.

35. U.S. Civil Service Commission, *Biography of an Ideal*, 71.

36. Wallace S. Sayre, "The Triumph of Techniques over Purpose," in *Classics of Public Personnel Policy*, edited by Frank J. Thompson, 2d ed. (Pacific Grove, Calif.: Brooks/Cole, 1991), 155.

37. U.S. Civil Service Commission, *Biography of an Ideal*, 77.

38. *The Hoover Commission Report* (New York: McGraw-Hill, 1949), vi.

39. Norton E. Long, "Power and Administration," *Public Administration Review* 9 (Autumn 1949): 257.

40. Mosher, *Democracy and the Public Service*, 3–4.

41. David T. Stanley, Dean E. Mann, and Jameson W. Doig, *Men Who Govern: A Biographical Profile of Federal Political Executives* (Washington, D.C.: Brookings Institution, 1967), 105.

Chapter Four: Adding On to the System

1. National Commission on the Public Service, *Leadership for America: Rebuilding the Public Service* (Lexington, Mass.: Lexington Books, 1990), 132.

2. For a discussion of the impact of the courts on one agency, see Rosemary O'Leary, *Environmental Change: Federal Courts and the EPA* (Philadelphia: Temple University Press, 1993).

3. Hugh M. Heclo, *A Government of Strangers: Executive Politics in Washington* (Washington, D.C.: Brookings Institution, 1977), 19.

4. National Performance Review, *Creating a Government*, 3.

5. U.S. Civil Service Commission, *Biography of an Ideal*, 78.

6. See George Milkovich and Alexandra Wigdor, eds., *Pay for Performance: Evaluating Performance Appraisal and Merit Pay* (Washington, D.C.: National Academy Press, 1991).

7. U.S. Civil Service Commission, *Biography of an Ideal*, 98–99.

8. National Commission on the Public Service, *Leadership for America*, 274.

9. Wilmerding, *Government by Merit*, 132.

10. Ibid., 141.

11. U.S. Civil Service Commission, *Biography of an Ideal*, 92.

12. Fesler and Kettl, *Politics of the Administrative Process*, 119.

13. See National Commission on the Public Service, "Report of the Task Force on Recruitment and Retention to the National Commission on the Public Service," in *Leadership for America: Rebuilding the Public Service* (Washington, D.C.: National Commission on the Public Service, 1989), 2:81.

14. See Carolyn Ban and Patricia W. Ingraham, "Retaining Quality Federal Employees: Life after PACE," *Public Administration Review* 48 (May–June 1988): 708–18. See also U.S. Merit Systems Protection Board, *In Search of Merit: Hiring Entry-Level Federal Employees* (Washington, D.C.: U.S. Government Printing Office, 1987).

15. National Commission on the Public Service, "Report of the Task Force on Recruitment and Retention," 81.

16. U.S. Office of Personnel Management, *Career America: College Relations and Recruitment Study* (Washington, D.C.: U.S. Office of Personnel Management, 1990), 1.

17. For a concise summary of relevant legislation, see Donald E. Klingner and John Nalbandian, *Public Personnel Management: Context and Strategies*, 3d ed. (Englewood Cliffs, N.J.: Prentice-Hall, 1993), 123.

18. For one perspective on this, see U.S. Civil Service Commission, *Biography of an Ideal*, 103–6 and 160–66.

19. Mosher, *Democracy and the Public Service*, 95. This assumes Mosher's "active" definition of representative bureaucracy. For a fuller discussion of this concept and his alternative definition, "passive" representation, see 10–14.

20. U.S. Civil Service Commission, *Biography of an Ideal*, 102.

21. *Griggs v. Duke Power Company*, 28 L Ed 2d 163 (1971).

22. Thompson, *Classics of Public Personnel Policy*, 229. See all of section 4, "Equal Employment Opportunity and Representation," for a more complete discussion of these issues.

23. Ibid., 231.

24. *Wards Cove Packing Company v. Frank Atonio*, 104 L Ed (1989).

25. See Elaine Johansen, *Comparable Worth: The Myth and the Movement* (Boulder, Colo.: Westview Press, 1984).

26. See Thomas A. DiPrete, *The Bureaucratic Labor Market: The Case of the Federal Civil Service* (New York: Plenum Press, 1989), and Sonia Ospina, "Job Classification and Organizational Mobility" (Ph.D. diss., State University of New York at Stony Brook, 1987).

27. See Kirke Harper, "The Senior Executive Service after One Decade," in *The Promise and Paradox of Civil Service Reform*, edited by Patricia W. Ingraham and David H. Rosenbloom (Pittsburgh: University of Pittsburgh Press, 1992), 274–75.

28. J. Edward Kellough and David H. Rosenbloom, "Representative Bureaucracy and the EEOC: Did Civil Service Reform Make a Difference?" in Ingraham and Rosenbloom, *Promise and Paradox*, 256–59.

29. U.S. Office of Personnel Management, Central Personnel Data File.

30. U.S. Office of Personnel Management, *The Status of the Senior Executive Service, 1991* (Washington, D.C.: U.S. Office of Personnel Management, 1992), 30.

31. For a thorough discussion of the early development of unions in the public sector, see Van Riper, *History*, 273–77 and 347–57.

32. Fesler and Kettl, *Politics of the Administrative Process*, 131.

33. Ibid., 130–33.

34. Van Riper, *History*, 380.

35. National Commission on the Public Service, "Report of the Task Force on Education and Training," in *Leadership for America* (1989 ed.), 2:143.

36. Donald F. Kettl, "Managing on the Frontiers of Knowledge: The Learning Organization," in Ingraham, Romzek, and Associates, *New Paradigms for Government*, 22.

37. Patricia W. Ingraham and David H. Rosenbloom, "The State of Merit

in the Federal Government," in Ingraham and Kettl, *Agenda for Excellence*, 285.

Chapter Five: Reforming the System

1. See the discussion of the expansion of the merit principles in Ingraham and Rosenbloom, "State of Merit," 289–91.

2. Ibid., 291.

3. See National Academy of Public Administration, *Revitalizing Federal Management: Managers and Their Overburdened Systems* (Washington, D.C.: National Academy of Public Administration, 1983).

4. James Q. Wilson, *Bureaucracy: What Government Agencies Do and Why They Do It* (New York: Basic Books, 1989), 217.

5. See Peters, *American Public Policy Process;* see also Meier, *Politics and the Bureaucracy.*

6. For excellent discussions of the congressional role in these efforts, see Paul C. Light, "Watch What We Pass: A Brief Legislative History of Civil Service Reform," in Ingraham and Rosenbloom, *Promise and Paradox,* 303–25, and Light, *The New Monitors: The Rise of Inspectors General, 1978–1990* (Washington, D.C.: Brookings Institution, 1992).

7. See Patricia W. Ingraham, "The Design of Civil Service Reform," in Ingraham and Rosenbloom, *Promise and Paradox,* 23.

8. Ibid., 20–23.

9. See Naomi B. Lynn and Richard E. Vaden, "Bureaucratic Response to Civil Service Reform," *Public Administration Review* 39 (July–August 1979): 333–43.

10. Ingraham, "Design of Civil Service Reform," 25.

11. Senate Committee on Governmental Affairs, *Statement of Dwight Ink before the Committee on Governmental Affairs: Hearings on the Civil Service Reform Act of 1978 and Reorganization Plan No. 2 of 1978,* 95th Cong., 2d sess., May 3, 1978.

12. In 1989 the Ethics in Government Act removed the Office of Special Counsel from the Merit Systems Protection Board and made it a separate agency.

13. James P. Pfiffner, "Political Appointees and Career Executives: The Democracy-Bureaucracy Nexus in the Twenty-First Century," *Public Administration Review* 47 (January–February 1987): 57. See also Mark W. Huddleston, "To the Threshold of Reform: The Senior Executive Service and America's Search for a Higher Civil Service," in Ingraham and Rosenbloom, *Promise and Paradox,* 165–98.

14. Some analysts argue that this 10 percent figure simply put into the legislation what had been practice for a long time. Chester Newland, for example, says that 10 to 12 percent of GS16–18 employees had traditionally been political. See Chester A. Newland, "The Politics of Civil Service Reform," in Ingraham and Rosenbloom, *Promise and Paradox,* 76–78.

15. Donald F. Parker, Susan J. Schurman, and B. Ruth Montgomery, "Labor-Management Relations under CSRA: Provisions and Effects," in *Legislating Bu-*

reaucratic Change: The Civil Service Reform Act of 1978, edited by Patricia W. Ingraham and Carolyn Ban (Albany: State University of New York Press, 1984), 163.

16. See the discussion of this issue by Chester Newland, the director of the Labor Relations Task Force of the Personnel Management Project, in Newland, "Politics of Civil Service Reform," 76–78. See also the report of that task force in *President's Personnel Management Project: Final Report.*

17. Alan K. Campbell, "Civil Service Reform: A New Commitment," *Public Administration Review* 38 (March–April 1978): 103.

18. Newland, "Politics of Civil Service Reform," 84.

19. Alan K. Campbell, remarks at the Symposium on Civil Service Reform, State University of New York at Binghamton, October 1981.

20. For additional discussion of this program, see David H. Rosenbloom and Curtis R. Berry, "The Civil Service Reform Act and EEO: The Record to Date," in Ingraham and Ban, *Legislating Bureaucratic Change,* 182–202.

21. Carolyn Ban, "Implementing Civil Service Reform," in Ingraham and Ban, *Legislating Bureaucratic Change,* 49.

22. Alan K. Campbell, "Revitalizing the Federal Personnel System," *Public Personnel Management* 7, no. 6 (January–February 1978): 59.

23. Campbell, "Civil Service Reform," 100.

24. Robert Vaughn, "The U.S. Merit Systems Protection Board," in Ingraham and Rosenbloom, *Promise and Paradox,* 122.

25. Ban, "Implementing Civil Service Reform," 52.

26. Alan K. Campbell, in comments before the Symposium on Civil Service Reform, State University of New York at Binghamton, October 1981.

27. See the discussion of this issue in Mark Huddleston, *The Government's Managers: Report of the Twentieth Century Fund's Task Force on the Senior Executive Service* (New York: Priority Press, 1987).

28. See U.S. General Accounting Office, *The Public Service: Issues Affecting Its Quality, Effectiveness, Integrity, and Stewardship* (Washington, D.C.: U.S. General Accounting Office, 1989), and U.S. Merit Systems Protection Board, *The Senior Executive Service: Views of Former Federal Executives* (Washington, D.C.: U.S. Merit Systems Protection Board, 1989).

29. See Gregory H. Gaertner, Karen N. Gaertner, and Irene Davis, "Federal Agencies in the Context of Transition: A Contrast between Democratic and Organizational Theories," *Public Administration Review* 43 (September–October 1983): 421–29.

30. See Karen N. Gaertner and Gregory H. Gaertner, "Performance Evaluation and Merit Pay: Results in the Environmental Protection Agency and the Mine Safety and Health Administration," in Ingraham and Ban, *Legislating Bureaucratic Change,* 87–111.

31. See E. E. Lawler, *Pay and Organization Development* (Reading, Mass.: Addison-Wesley, 1981), and Victor Vroom, *Work and Motivation* (New York: Wiley, 1964).

32. Gaertner and Gaertner, "Performance Evaluation and Merit Pay," 110.

33. See Jone L. Pearce and James L. Perry, "Federal Merit Pay: A Longitudinal Analysis," *Public Administration Review* 43 (September–October 1983): 315–25, and Jone L. Pearce, William B. Stevenson, and James L. Perry, "Managerial Compensation Based on Organizational Performance: A Time Series Analysis of the Impact of Merit Pay," *Academy of Management Journal* 28 (June 1985): 261–78.

34. See U.S. Merit Systems Protection Board, *Performance Management and Recognition System: Linking Pay to Performance* (Washington, D.C.: U.S. Merit Systems Protection Board, 1987), and James L. Perry, "The Merit Pay Reforms," in Ingraham and Rosenbloom, *Promise and Paradox*, 201–5.

35. See Perry, "Merit Pay Reforms," and U.S. Office of Personnel Management, *Performance Management and Recognition System* (Washington, D.C.: U.S. Office of Personnel Management, 1987, 1988, 1989).

36. For a thorough discussion of these issues, see the study commissioned by the OPM from the National Academy of Science: Milkovich and Wigdor, *Pay for Performance.*

37. U.S. Office of Personnel Management, *Final Report of the Joint Labor-Management Committee on Pay for Performance* (Washington, D.C.: U.S. Office of Personnel Management, 1992).

38. See, as examples of OPM publications on this subject, *Status of the Evaluation of the Navy Personnel Management Demonstration Project: Report #1* (Washington, D.C.: U.S. Office of Personnel Management, 1984), and *Results of Title VI Demonstration Projects: Implications for Performance Management and Pay for Performance* (Washington, D.C.: U.S. Office of Personnel Management, 1991). See also Carolyn Ban, "Research and Demonstrations under CSRA," in Ingraham and Rosenbloom, *Promise and Paradox*, 217–35, and Organization for Economic Cooperation and Development, *Private Pay for Public Work* (Paris: Organization for Economic Cooperation and Development, 1993), 78–83.

39. U.S. Office of Personnel Management, *Results of Title VI Demonstration Projects.*

40. U.S. General Accounting Office, *Observations on the Navy's Personnel Demonstration Project* (Washington, D.C.: U.S. General Accounting Office, 1988).

41. U.S. Office of Personnel Management, *Results of Title VI Demonstration Projects.*

42. See the National Academy of Public Administration, *Modernizing Federal Classification: An Opportunity for Excellence* (Washington, D.C.: National Academy of Public Administration, 1991).

43. See Brigitte W. Schay, *Broad-Banding in the Federal Government: Management Report* (Washington, D.C.: U.S. Office of Personnel Management, 1993).

44. This term is from Gregory H. Gaertner and Karen N. Gaertner, "Civil Service Reform in the Context of Presidential Transitions," in Ingraham and Ban, *Legislating Bureaucratic Change*, 218–44.

45. Devine, "Political Administration," 125–35.

46. Larry M. Lane, "The Office of Personnel Management," in Ingraham and Rosenbloom, *Promise and Paradox*, 109.

Chapter Six: Presidential Management Strategies

1. "Report of the President's Committee," 114.

2. Kaufman, "Administrative Decentralization."

3. Devine, "Political Administration," 129.

4. Mosher, *Democracy and the Public Service*, 3. For a more recent discussion of these same issues, see "Forum on Public Administration."

5. For a discussion of the emergent role of bureaucracy, see B. Guy Peters, *American Public Policy: Problems and Prospects*, 2d ed. (Chatham, N.J.: Chatham House, 1992). See also Lewis C. Mainzer and Francis E. Rourke, *Bureaucratic Power in National Policy Making: Readings*, 4th ed. (Boston: Little, Brown, 1986).

6. Gaertner and Gaertner, "Civil Service Reform," 221.

7. Frederick Malek (for the White House Personnel Office) in a memorandum commonly referred to as the "Malek Manual," in *Public Personnel Administration*, edited by Frank J. Thompson (Oak Park, Ill.: Moore, 1979), 160.

8. See the discussion in Patricia W. Ingraham, "Commissions, Cycles, and Change," in Ingraham and Kettl, *Agenda for Excellence*, 187–207. See also Arnold, *Making the Managerial Presidency*.

9. Joel D. Aberbach and Bert A. Rockman, "Clashing Beliefs within the Executive Branch: The Nixon Administration Bureaucracy," *American Political Science Review* 70 (June 1976): 456–68.

10. See Barbara S. Romzek and J. Stephen Hendriks, "Organizational Involvement and Representative Bureaucracy: Can We Have It Both Ways?" *American Political Science Review* 76 (March 1982): 75–82; Barbara S. Romzek, "Employee Investment and Commitment: The Ties That Bind," *Public Administration Review* 50 (May–June 1990): 374–82; and James L. Perry and Lois Recascino Wise, "The Motivational Bases of Public Service," *Public Administration Review* 50 (May–June 1990): 367–73.

11. See National Committee on the Public Service, "Report of the Task Force on Recruitment and Retention."

12. Patricia W. Ingraham, "Political Direction and Policy Change in Three Federal Agencies," in *The Managerial Presidency*, edited by James P. Pfiffner (Pacific Grove, Calif.: Brooks/Cole, 1991), 190.

13. See Seidman and Gilmour, *Politics, Position, and Power*, 98.

14. Richard M. Nixon, "Annual Message to the Congress on the State of the Union, January 22, 1971," in *Public Papers of the Presidents of the United States: Richard Nixon, 1971* (Washington, D.C.: U.S. Government Printing Office, 1972), 51.

15. For a more complete discussion, see Arnold, *Making the Managerial Presidency*, and John Hart, *The Presidential Branch* (New York: Pergamon Press, 1987).

16. James P. Pfiffner, *The Strategic Presidency: Hitting the Ground Running* (Chicago: Dorsey Press, 1988), 50, 81. See also Richard P. Nathan, *The Plot That Failed: Nixon and the Administrative Presidency* (New York: Wiley, 1975).

17. See James P. Pfiffner, *The President, the Budget, and Congress: Impoundment and the 1974 Budget Act* (Boulder, Colo.: Westview Press, 1979), and, for the illegal use of the merit system, House Committee on Post Office and Civil Service, *Violations and Abuses of Merit Principles in Federal Employment: Hearings before the Subcommittee on Manpower and Civil Service,* part 1, 94th Cong., 1st sess., April 10, 1975.

18. Pfiffner, *Strategic Presidency,* 53. See also Richard E. Neustadt, *Presidential Power: The Politics of Leadership from FDR to Carter* (New York: Wiley, 1980).

19. See Pfiffner, *Strategic Presidency,* 107–8.

20. See the discussion of the Federal Executive Service in Huddleston, "To The Threshold of Reform," 175–78.

21. Whether pay-for-performance systems ever achieve these ends is another matter. See George Milkovich and Alexandra Wigdor, eds., *Performance Appraisal and Merit Pay* (Washington, D.C.: National Research Council, 1991), for a private-sector and American perspective; for an international perspective, see Organization for Economic Cooperation and Development, *Private Pay for Public Work.*

22. See Terry Moe, "The Politicized Presidency," in *The New Direction in American Politics,* edited by John Chubb and Paul Peterson (Washington, D.C.: Brookings Institution, 1985), 260–72.

23. Heclo, *Government of Strangers,* 154.

24. G. Calvin Mackenzie, "Cabinet and Subcabinet Personnel Selection in Reagan's First Year: New Variations on Some Not So Old Themes" (paper presented at the Annual Meeting of the American Political Science Association, New York, 1981).

25. See Rector and Sanera, *Steering the Elephant,* and Sanera, "Implementing the Mandate," in ibid., 457–560.

26. Ibid, 514.

27. Chester A. Newland, "A Midterm Appraisal—The Reagan Presidency: Limited Government and Political Administration," *Public Administration Review* 43 (January–February 1983): 2.

28. Ingraham, "Building Bridges or Burning Them?" 429.

29. U.S. House of Representatives Subcommittee on Civil Service, news releases, "Number of Political Appointees Up, Careerists Down in Federal Central Management Agencies," April 18, 1985, and "Plum Book Shows More Political Appointees in Reagan Administration Than in Carter Administration," April 24, 1985.

30. See the discussion in Ingraham, "Political Direction and Policy Change."

31. See the discussion of HUD in Hal G. Rainey, *Understanding and Managing Public Organizations* (San Francisco: Jossey-Bass, 1991), 73–75.

32. James P. Pfiffner, "Establishing the Bush Presidency," *Public Administration Review* 50 (January–February 1990): 64.

33. President Bush recommended a salary increase for top executives in 1989; that recommendation was approved by Congress, but the link between executive-level employees and members of Congress was maintained.

34. Pfiffner, "Establishing the Bush Presidency," 69. For additional discussion, see Patricia W. Ingraham, James R. Thompson, and Elliot F. Eisenberg, "Political Management Strategies and Political/Career Relationships: Where Are We Now in the Federal Government?" *Public Administration Review* 55 (May–June 1995).

35. U.S. Office of Personnel Management, *The Senior Executive Service* (Washington, D.C.: U.S. Office of Personnel Management, 1989), 1.

36. Data from the Office of Staffing Policy and Evaluations, U.S. Office of Personnel Management, March 1993.

37. Ingraham, Thompson, and Eisenberg, "Political Management Strategies."

38. National Performance Review, *Creating a Government*.

39. These figures do not include military or foreign-service personnel, ambassadors, appointees to international organizations, or members of the Public Health Service or White House staff. See Ingraham, "Building Bridges or Burning Them?" 427, and the excellent discussion in Fesler and Kettl, *Politics of the Administrative Process,* chapter 7.

40. See, for example, the discussion of the Bush presidency in Pfiffner, "Establishing the Bush Presidency," and the discussion of the Reagan administration in Ingraham, "Political Direction and Policy Change."

41. Heclo, *Government of Strangers.*

42. National Commission on the Public Service, "Report of the Task Force on the Relations between Political Appointees and Career Executives to the National Commission on the Public Service," in *Leadership for America* (1990 ed.), 220.

43. See, for example, Mackenzie, *In-and-Outers.*

44. Fesler and Kettl, *Politics of the Administrative Process,* 153.

45. See, for example, Rosabeth Moss Kanter, *The Change Masters: Innovation for Productivity in the American Corporation* (New York: Simon and Schuster, 1983), and Karen N. Gaertner, "Managers' Careers and Organizational Change," *Academy of Management Executives* 4 (1988): 311–18.

46. Paul C. Light, "When Worlds Collide: The Political-Career Nexus," in Mackenzie, *In-and-Outers,* 156–73.

47. Ingraham, "Political Direction and Policy Change."

48. Ronald P. Sanders, "Reinventing the Senior Executive Service," in Ingraham, Romzek, and Associates, *New Paradigms for Government,* 215–38.

49. James P. Pfiffner, "Political Appointees and Career Executives: The Democracy-Bureaucracy Nexus," in Ingraham and Kettl, *Agenda for Excellence,* 57–58.

50. Ibid., 59.

51. Newland, "Politics of Civil Service Reform," 64.

52. Joel D. Aberbach and Bert A. Rockman, "Political and Bureaucratic Roles in Public Service Reorganization," in *Organizing Governance: Governing Organizations,* edited by Colin Campbell and B. Guy Peters (Pittsburgh: University of Pittsburgh Press, 1988), 1.

53. Rosenbloom and Ross argue that these administrative controls, particularly those contained in the 1946 Administrative Procedures Act, demonstrate that Congress has had a long-term strategy for maintaining its presence in the bureaucratic management arena. For a full discussion of this position, see Rosenbloom and Ross, "Administrative Theory," 145–67.

54. Light, "Watch What We Pass," 314.

55. Ibid., 307.

56. Paul C. Light, "An End to the War on Waste," *Brookings Review* (April 1993): 48. For the full analysis, see Light, *Monitoring Government: Inspectors General and the Search for Accountability* (Washington, D.C.: Brookings Institution, 1993).

57. Norman J. Ornstein, Thomas Mann, and Michael Malbin, *Vital Statistics on Congress: 1991–1992* (Washington, D.C.: American Enterprise Institute, 1992); see also Mark Bisnow, *In the Shadow of the Dome: Chronicles of a Capitol Hill Aide* (New York: William Morrow, 1990).

58. Donald F. Kettl, "Micromanagement: Congressional Control and Bureaucratic Risk," in Ingraham and Kettl, *Agenda for Excellence*, 98.

59. Burdette Loomis, *The New American Politician: Ambition, Entrepreneurship, and the Changing Face of Political Life* (New York: Basic Books, 1988).

60. Kettl, "Micromanagement," 106.

Chapter Seven: Changing Work, Changing Workforce, Changing Expectations

1. For a discussion of this issue, see National Commission on the Public Service, "Report of the Task Force on Recruitment and Retention."

2. See Margo Bailey, "The Reality of the Glass Ceiling for African-Americans in the Federal Civil Service" (Ph.D. diss., Maxwell School, Syracuse University, 1995).

3. Donald F. Kettl, *Sharing Power: Public Governance and Private Markets* (Washington, D.C.: Brookings Institution, 1993), 17.

4. National Performance Review, *Creating a Government*, 1.

5. Ibid., i.

6. See the discussion of these changes and shifting influences in Mosher, *Democracy and the Public Service*, chapter 2.

7. Wilmerding, *Government by Merit*, 17–18.

8. Charles H. Levine and Rosslyn S. Kleeman, "The Quiet Crisis in the American Public Service," in Ingraham and Kettl, *Agenda for Excellence*, 214.

9. Ibid., 215–16.

10. For a discussion of the need for "learning organizations," see Kettl, "Managing on the Frontiers of Knowledge," 19–40.

11. See Donald F. Kettl, *Government by Proxy: (Mis)Managing Federal Programs* (Washington, D.C.: Congressional Quarterly Press, 1988).

12. Kettl, *Sharing Power*, 9.

13. H. Brinton Milward, "Implications of Contracting Out: New Roles for the Hollow State," in Ingraham, Romzek, and Associates, *New Paradigms for Government*, 41–62.

14. Ibid., 6.

15. Kettl, *Sharing Power*, 204.

16. See Milward, "Implications of Contracting Out."

17. Howard N. Fullerton, "Labor Force Projections: The Baby Boom Moves On," *Monthly Labor Review* (November 1991): 31.

18. Ibid., 40–41.

19. Levine, "Federal Government in the Year 2000," 176.

20. See U.S. Office of Personnel Management, "Affirmative Employment Statistics" (Washington, D.C.: U.S. Office of Personnel Management, September 1990), 4–7.

21. See Michael V. Reagen, "Shifting Demographic and Social Realities," in *Handbook of Public Administration*, edited by James L. Perry (San Francisco: Jossey-Bass, 1989), 72.

22. U.S. General Accounting Office, "The Changing Workforce: Demographic Issues Facing the Federal Government" (Washington, D.C.: U.S. Government Printing Office, 1992), 25.

23. Ibid., 24.

24. Ibid., 65. The number of federal employees in the age group from thirty-five to forty-four grew more rapidly in the period from 1976 to 1990 than did that age group in the workforce generally, increasing from 66 percent to slightly more than 74 percent.

25. U.S. Office of Personnel Management, *Civil Service 2000* (Washington, D.C.: U.S. Government Printing Office, 1988), 32.

26. U.S. General Accounting Office, "Employment Policy Challenges Created by an Aging Workforce" (Washington, D.C.: U.S. General Accounting Office, 1993), 8.

27. Ibid., 3.

28. It must be noted that the reinvention teams were composed largely of career civil servants, even though overall direction and coordination was provided by staff to Vice President Gore. Further, there were reinvention teams inside each federal department, and these, too, were primarily career efforts.

29. See James R. Thompson and Patricia W. Ingraham, "Organizational Redesign in the Public Sector: Theory and Reality," in *The State of Public Management*, edited by Donald F. Kettl and H. Brinton Milward (Baltimore: Johns Hopkins University Press, 1995), for a discussion of these reengineering reforms.

30. For a full discussion and complete list of Osborne and Gaebler's principles for reinvention, see Osborne and Gaebler, *Reinventing Government*. For a response to Osborne and Gaebler, see John J. DiIulio, Jr., Gerald Garvey, and Donald F. Kettl, *Improving Government Performance: An Owner's Manual* (Washington, D.C.: Brookings Institution, 1993).

31. National Performance Review, *Creating a Government*, 7.

32. General Charles G. Dawes, in his first address to the Congress, quoted in Gawthrop, *Administrative Process and Democratic Theory*, 93–95.

33. Donald F. Kettl, *Reinventing Government? Appraising the National Performance Review* (Washington, D.C.: Brookings Institution, 1994), 48.

34. National Performance Review, *Creating a Government*, 8–9.

35. U.S. General Accounting Office, "Comments on NPR's Recommendations" (Washington, D.C.: U.S. General Accounting Office, 1993), 3.

36. For additional discussion of the "management side" of the OMB, see Beryl A. Radin, "The Search for the 'M': Federal Management and Personnel Policy," in Ingraham and Rosenbloom, *Promise and Paradox*, 37–62.

Chapter Eight: Transforming Merit

1. Wilson, *Bureaucracy*, 377.

2. Nelson, "Short, Ironic History," 774.

3. Michael Barzelay, *Breaking through Bureaucracy: A New Vision for Managing Government* (Berkeley and Los Angeles: University of California Press, 1992), 120.

4. For a discussion, see Ingraham and Rosenbloom, "Political Foundations."

5. Kettl, *Sharing Power.*

6. U.S. General Accounting Office, *Program Performance Measures: Federal Collection and Use of Performance Data* (Washington, D.C.: U.S. Government Printing Office, 1992).

7. National Performance Review, *Creating a Government*, 72.

8. See Thompson and Ingraham, "Organizational Redesign."

9. Michael Hammer and James Champy, *Re-engineering the Corporation: A Manifesto for Business Revolution* (New York: HarperBusiness, 1993), 34.

10. For an excellent discussion of this problem, see Mark Abramson and Richard Schmidt, "Implementing the Civil Service Reform Act in a Time of Turbulence," in Ingraham and Ban, *Legislating Bureaucratic Change*, 245–53.

11. See Thompson and Ingraham, "Organizational Redesign."

12. See, for example, the discussion in National Performance Review, *Reinventing Government Summit Proceedings* (Washington, D.C.: National Performance Review, 1993).

13. This summary is derived from W. Edwards Deming, *Out of the Crisis* (Cambridge, Mass.: MIT Center for Advanced Engineering Study, 1986).

14. DiIulio, Garvey, and Kettl, *Improving Government Performance*, 63.

15. See Ingraham and Rosenbloom, "State of Merit," 274–96.

16. The classic statement of the debate is the dialogue between Carl J. Friedrich and Herman Finer; see Friedrich, "Public Policy and the Nature of Administrative Responsibility," in *Public Policy, 1940*, edited by C. J. Friedrich and Edward S. Mason (Cambridge, Mass.: Harvard University Press, 1940), and Herman Finer, "Administrative Responsibility and Democratic Governance," *Public Administration Review* 1 (Summer 1941): 335–50.

17. Barbara S. Romzek and Melvin J. Dubnick, "Issues of Accountability in Flexible Personnel Systems," in Ingraham, Romzek, and Associates, *New Paradigms for Government*, 263–94.

18. Ibid., 271–72.

19. Ibid., 288.

20. For a discussion of public service commitment, see Perry and Wise, "Moti-

vational Bases of Public Service." For a discussion of an accountability mechanism related directly to public service employment, see Rohr, *To Run a Constitution*. Rohr argues that taking the oath of office creates constitutional accountability.

21. For a more extensive discussion, see Ingraham, "Of Pigs in Pokes."

22. See Thompson and Ingraham, "Organizational Redesign."

Index